Praise for

Something Old, Something New

"A lovely and literary cookbook . . . handsome and witty and personal, full of glimpses into Adler's life."

—Vogue.com

"Home cooks looking to adventure into the past will find much to enjoy with these refound recipes."

—*Library Journal* (starred review)

"Reimagines emblematic continental fare and famous chef-inspired dishes of a bygone era, breathing new life into more than 100 culinary mainstays. . . . Adler's beautiful, reflective prose provides history and insight into each dish and she shows how nostalgic, old school dishes can taste current when remade with a modern sensibility."

—*Publishers Weekly*

"Adler has a curious intelligence and technical command to back up a thoughtful approach to classic French dishes, which reimagines what might be produced out of a home kitchen. . . . Any cook looking to exercise and enhance creativity will find in Adler a worthy muse."

—*Booklist*

"Revitalizes fusty classics and long-forgotten dishes, bringing them into this century with verve and ease. . . . It's bookery meets cookery."

—Christine Muhlke, *Bon Appétit*

"A personal, nostalgic journey inspiring the rediscovery of classics . . . As much about the writing as it is about the cooking . . . Lyrical."

—Jenny Rosenstrach, *The New York Times Book Review*

"Adler wins readers over with an encouraging voice that eschews preciousness. Her recipes are hardly strict or precise. They are approachable and acknowledge her rare quality among her class of chefs: frugality. . . . Her intimate knowledge of food and the way it reacts and performs has coalesced into a true instinct."

—Ayden LeRoux, *Los Angeles Review of Books*

"Unearths and modernizes culinary classics."

—Sierra Tishgart, *Grub Street*

"Demands to be languorously relished."

—Shira Feder, *Forward*

"Inspires a resurrection and revival, just as much as a revision of, classic recipes."

—*Apiece Apart*

"Whether it's cooking with leftovers or modernizing dishes that've been tossed to the wayside over the years, she has a clear appreciation for that which might otherwise be taken for granted in a culture of excess."

—Megan Burns, *Brightest Young Things*

"Old-school foods made modern not by invention but by translation: by determining what in the original recipes was worth keeping and re-creating it in a contemporary kitchen for contemporary eaters. . . . Set in prose as weaving and lucid as a walk in the park."

—Caroline Lange, *Edible Manhattan*

"Tamar Adler is more than a wonderful food writer—she is a wonderful writer. She delves into these past and forgotten recipes with the spirit of an adventurer and a sleuth, and while writing about food, she is always secretly writing about something else—a love of life, eternal values, industry, thrift, friendship, the unknown. Her books—written with a charmingly loose confidence and care—feel timeless. Even those of us who never cook, or don't give meals much thought, will find enduring literary pleasure in *Something Old, Something New*."

—Sheila Heti, author of *How Should a Person Be?*

"What a delight this book is. It reminded me of half-forgotten treats and made me nostalgic for things I've never actually tasted. But most of all, I treasure *Something Old, Something New* for the writing, which is as suave and fun to read as M. F. K. Fisher. Adler is the best kind of kitchen companion, someone whose warm and witty voice I want to carry with me as I cook."

—Bee Wilson, author of *Consider the Fork*

"Tamar Adler is a curious magpie, skillfully collecting culinary ephemera from across the ages and weaving them into an unimaginably beautiful nest. Step inside. You'll find yourself comforted and inspired by the writing and the food, both equally sensible and elegant."

—Samin Nosrat, author of *Salt, Fat, Acid, Heat*

"Tamar Adler is a special pleasure—from the intensity of her interest to her keen observations and joy in language. When she looks at half-forgotten delicious dishes, she makes them seem as fresh as morning."

—Ed Behr, editor, *The Art of Eating*

"A wonderful new book by one of my favorite food writers."

—@MichaelPollan

ALSO BY TAMAR ADLER

An Everlasting Meal

Something Old, Something New

Oysters Rockefeller, Walnut Soufflé,
and Other Classic Recipes Revisited

Tamar Adler

SCRIBNER

New York   London   Toronto   Sydney   New Delhi

Scribner
An Imprint of Simon & Schuster, Inc.
1230 Avenue of the Americas
New York, NY 10020

First Scribner trade paperback edition August 2019

SCRIBNER and design are registered trademarks of The Gale Group, Inc.,
used under license by Simon & Schuster, Inc., the publisher of this work.

For information about special discounts for bulk purchases,
please contact Simon & Schuster Special Sales at 1-866-506-1949
or business@simonandschuster.com.

The Simon & Schuster Speakers Bureau can bring authors to your live event.
For more information or to book an event, contact the Simon & Schuster Speakers
Bureau at 1-866-248-3049 or visit our website at www.simonspeakers.com.

Manufactured in the United States of America

1   3   5   7   9   10   8   6   4   2

Library of Congress Control Number: 2018288729

ISBN 978-1-4767-9961-2
ISBN 978-1-9821-1399-5 (pbk)
ISBN 978-1-4767-9964-3 (ebook)

For Peter,
whose Yankee constitution
was corrupted with cream in the making of these pages,
and who bore it with bravery and love

Is there anything of which one can say, *"Look! This is something new?"*

It was here already, long ago; it was here before our time.

—Ecclesiastes 1:10

CONTENTS

Menu for a Fancy Spring Dinner

LA BONNE SOUPE (Soups)

Menu for a Summer Lunch

A GROWING LOVE (Salads)

Menu for a Fancy Summer Dinner

IN VEGETABLE VERITAS (Vegetables)

Menu for an Autumn Lunch

TO RISE LIKE RICE (Starches and Eggs)

Menu for a Fast Autumn Dinner

A GOOD EFFECT (Meat)

Menu for an Early Winter Dinner

ON POVERTY AND OYSTERS (Seafood)

Menu for a Late-Winter Dinner

CRYING FOR CREAM (Desserts)

ALCOHOLIC APPENDIX (A Few Drinks) 243

INTRODUCTION

Some years ago I found myself drafted into service, at first only dimly consciously, by culinary inventions I encountered in old cookbooks or on menus. They sounded elegant and subtle, or fantastical, or basic and rugged and good, but for one reason or another not reproducible in my own kitchen today. Reflexively, I collected them and did what I could to give them a second life.

Eventually I had a bookful. None had passed out of use because it was *bad*, but because the passage of time prompts inevitable changes: in the language of kitchen instruction, and in fashion, and in us. We and the world reorganize ourselves regularly, and the recipes of one era are left behind at the dawn of the next. Some of those that enlisted me were mired in old language—the word "boil" once meant "cook"; now it refers specifically to a liquid joggling with bubbles at 212 degrees; "scallop" meant either a way of cutting or broiling under a hot flame; now it is only a hopping mollusk. Some come from forgotten days when seafood and vegetables in cans and Ritz crackers were considered modern and fresh fish and vegetables and coarse bread atavistic, or when meat was bathed in bottles of Burgundy as though, to crib from Charles Lamb, wine were "as cheap as dish water." Some, owing to the cuisine they imitated, leaned so heavily on butter and cream they lost their balance. In other instances, perfectly practical culinary habits slipped out loose pocket seams and blew errantly away.

As I gathered examples of each case, I repeated an eventually maniacal mantra: *This will be delicious when made anew with less butter, less wine, less time, less cost!*

That is how and why I wrote this book.

I also found intelligence, grace, and common sense in the wording of much older culinary advice as it was.

This I have included verbatim. It possesses perspective and often prose too good to change. For example, Rufus Estes's turn-of-the-century deliberations on lunch: "Yesterday's dinner perhaps consisted of roast turkey, beef or lamb, and there is some meat left over; then pick out one of my receipts calling for minced or creamed meats; baked or stuffed potatoes are always nice, or there may be cold potatoes left over that can be mashed, made into cakes and fried." Recipes from similar sages of a similar age contain, as well, what Oronte Churm calls a poetry of lost specifics. I trust their points of view and poetry to explain why I was so drawn to certain particularly old preparations that are nearly extinct, or very far down the dark hallway, toes up—and why I so want to help them back to their wobbly feet. Also for poetic and practical purposes, there are perceptive illustrations by Mindy Dubin and wine pairings by the regal Juliette Pope.

The third reason for this funny little cookbook is what made it a good fit for me. I am a lazy cook. Though I once did it professionally, I do not take *kitchen work* seriously. I am frugal, at least compared to the voluptuary souls whose recipes I've revised. In other words, though I did not mean specifically to make a book of old-fashioned dishes for faster times, that is what it became.

What was once precise is now estimated, what once took four steps now takes one (or two). If a shortcut exists, I have found it, out of blunt habit. Any technique that demanded too much seriousness has been unsentimentally removed, any effects that demanded true precision abandoned in favor of resiliency. This instinctual pragmatism has affected the selection of recipes. If any couldn't withstand my somewhat truculent treatment, it was excluded. If I caused those I did include any systemic harm, it was in spite of an almost Hippocratic will to avoid it. And, in the end, if dishes seem difficult, I venture that it is because they are unfamiliar: they are old, and so, new.

This may read as an apologia for all sorts of heresies. Whether the turning of coq au vin into chicken in leftover wine, salmon croquettes into salt cod ones, and baked Alaska into a stale-cake-perched ice cream bombe are acts of cultural preservation or crimes depends on how you, yourself, think things should be kept.

I believe that things must be used. That means accruing stains, enduring modifications. I think all of these recipes can, moreover, endure further modification and staining. I hope that in whatever kitchen, in whatever era, they find themselves, they're given the chance.

If I am very lucky and a little successful, this book will do something to restore the pleasures of restoration itself. Then, once the inevitable creakiness sets in, a new restorer will arrive and prop things up.

I have found the hours with these old-new friends a pleasant way to spend my time. I hope the evidence of that enjoyment is in these pages. It is a gratifying thing to read about antiquated habits and balms, but it is even more gratifying to keep the good things alive, and perhaps most gratifying to revive those already gone.

A SIMPLE
SPRING LUNCH

Pickled eggs

Crisp fish meunière

Petits pois à la française

Little boiled potatoes

Wine: A light, bright, lively, and barely
sweet young white
Example: Riesling
Peter Lauer Barrel X Riesling 2015

Tipsy cake

WHEN YOU ARE FAMISHED

Hors d'Œuvres

I

Famished people must be slowly nursed,
And fed by spoonfuls, else they always burst.
—Lord Byron, *Don Juan*, Canto II

I once attended a dinner hosted by the heiress of the Taittinger Champagne chateau, which began with a wild platter of crudités— crisp, raw vegetables regularly served before meals in years past. These were also known, at different tables, as "relish plates," in which case they consisted of *California* olives and celery—a combination I, a child who considered the act of eating diabolical, found irresistible, *if* they were cold. The heiress's arrangement included purple tendrils of amaranth, strangely shaped raw young zucchini, tiny mouse melons (which are a kind of cucumber), tomatoes the size of marbles. But crudités can be simpler and are inherently elegant and frugal and demand no equipment other than a knife. For a relaxed undertaking, one might consult the crudités primer in Richard Olney's 1970 *The French Menu Cookbook*:

> *Crudités* can be any combination of fresh, tender, young, raw vegetables: tiny, white heads of cauliflower, little radishes, the small, elongated, light green, sweet Italian peppers . . . hearts of celery, cherry tomatoes, scallions (if they are not too strong), bulb fennel, Belgian endives, avocados . . .

I have a few quibbles: even the tiniest white heads of cauliflower are digestively disruptive unless boiled in very salty water, then drained and chilled—rendering them no longer *cru*, but *cuit*. But then they

5

are delicious, and as refreshing as a dip in a pool. Fresh green beans and even broccoli might be included, as long as they, too, are boiled in salty water and allowed to cool first. I don't agree with Mr. Olney either about cherry tomatoes—which are too roly-poly for crudités, and I think best cut and mixed for a salad with half their volume of basil, a scattering of fresh spring onion, a good deal of salt, and a pour of red wine vinegar—or raw scallions, which I would not serve to anyone I would serve at will.

To his list, I add the mellowest olives—the ones that taste buttery; the crispest celery, lightly peeled if it's the pretty dark green branches found at farmers' markets; thin-skinned cucumbers (a disagreeable quality in humans being desirable in vegetables), cut on a diagonal; slivers of fennel; and, for the short months they're available, fava beans, served in their pods for eaters to pop out.

The only rule I can think of is to include radishes, which are uniquely lovely to look at and surprising to taste, if you can find good ones. What's a good one? There is no answer better than Marion Harland's in her 1871 *Commonsense Cookery*: "Good radishes are crisp to the teeth, look cool, and taste hot."

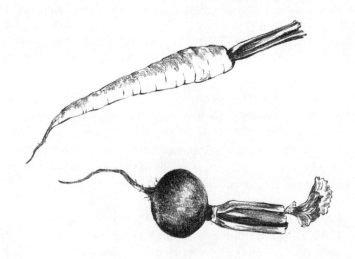

Then, you can serve your crudités, as the dark-jacketed waiters did at the Four Seasons, on dishes of chipped ice. Each vegetable will stay crisp and cool as a good radish and look like a shimmering jewel. I'm too thrifty with ice and time to do this, and resort to a large, pretty platter, but I still believe it to sometimes be fun to expend the energies to make raw vegetables look so bright and enticing. Or, go a different route entirely, giving each little cluster of cauliflower or cucumber its own bowl, and letting each sing its own song.

The mid-twentieth-century ascendancy of sauces as dips may be in part to blame for crudités' vanishing. Sauces took over as the thing that mattered, and the very thing that *did* matter—good vegetables— became an afterthought. There is irony to serving a dish alongside its executioner (and they don't really need any sauce but salt) but crudités do sometimes like a simple sauce nonetheless.

Here is one I learned to make on a desolate, hot Vietnamese beach fifteen years ago, where it was served with freshly boiled blue crabs. Both crab and sauce were bought for us by gangsters with long fingernails, who also served us moonshine from glass flasks. (I add of narrative compulsion that one carried a gun. Late that night we heard them at our hostel window, mewing like cats for us to come out to play.)

I call this Lime Sauce. To make it, put 2 parts kosher salt to 1 part freshly ground black pepper in a shallow bowl or teacup. Squeeze fresh lime juice over. Stop adding lime juice when it becomes a light sludge and taste it on a piece of cucumber or radish or whatever is in your crudités. Continue to add lime juice and make it as thin or thick as you like. This sauce looks murky but tastes piquant and clear.

I often serve the same three-ingredient mixture with boiled eggs or quail eggs, with or without crudités, and the aura of the Vietnamese gangsters hanging with appealing menace about my inner atmosphere.

Ravigote sauce is nearly as primitive. It is a rough mayonnaise-like mixture that was once a regular companion to chilled cucumbers and artichokes. It is startlingly simple and delicious. This one closely follows a recipe by Henry Harris, of the now departed Racine in London.

RAVIGOTE SAUCE

¼ teaspoon kosher salt
1 tablespoon finely chopped spring onion or shallot
4 teaspoons smooth Dijon mustard
1 tablespoon white wine vinegar
¼ to ½ egg yolk
½ cup vegetable oil
1 tablespoon chopped cornichons or other good pickle
2 tablespoons chopped fresh parsley
1 tablespoon chopped fresh chervil, lovage, tarragon, or celery
    leaves
freshly ground black pepper

Add the salt to the spring onion and let sit for 10 minutes. Whisk the mustard, vinegar, and yolk together in a bowl. Add the spring onions. Whisk again, and then very, very slowly, starting drop by drop and proceeding to a thin, even stream, whisk in the oil. Once completely emulsified, add the rest of the ingredients and taste for seasoning.

If the *ravigote* happens to break rather than stay in a smooth emulsion, put it back together by starting with a teaspoon of mustard and a bit of yolk in another bowl, then slowly whisk the broken sauce into it, as if it were oil, adding a little more oil as you finish. Alternatively and even more safely, put a large spoonful of crème fraîche or sour cream or heavy cream into a bowl. Then add a dab of mustard, a sprinkle of vinegar, and all the rest. Adjust the seasoning at the end of either procedure, and the sauce will be good as new.

Two alternative crudités sauces are herb mayonnaise—made by simply adding handfuls of finely chopped mixed herbs and a squeeze of freshening lemon to homemade or purchased mayonnaise—and almost-warm anchovy butter—made by roughly chopping good anchovies and mixing them into softened sweet butter.

There are a number of other old-fashioned hors d'œuvres that were composed in eminent good sense. A sampling so fine it is worth pinning up verbatim in any welcoming kitchen comes from Jules Gouffé, *chef de cuisine* of the Jockey Club in Paris, in his 1867 *Le livre de cuisine*:

Gherkins
Black radish, peeled, sliced, and salted
Green olives
Cucumber, sliced and salted, with *ravigote* (from the middle of
    April to the end of September)
Artichokes à la poivrade with oil and vinegar, pepper and salt
Anchovies in oil
Sardines in oil, garnished with parsley and capers
Pickled herrings in oil, with parsley and capers
Pickled oysters with fresh parsley
Mixed pickles

On M. Gouffé's list, acidity is the rule. One encounters there an old culinary wisdom that is still fresh and true today: strong-flavored preserved morsels dressed in new vinegar or lemon juice and oil are a consummate pre-dinner enticement, placing low demand on both cook and eater.

It is tempting to update each of Gouffé's suggestions. It would be an indulgence, though, and moreover unneeded. There is already a recipe for *ravigote*. All the others that aren't olives or pickles are slants on one culinary principle, best absorbed via a recipe for vegetables *à la grecque*.

Vegetables *à la grecque* is a combination of vegetables, often including white mushrooms and crisp celery, cooked quickly in oil and vinegar and cooled directly in their flavorful bath. It is a wonderful mostly forgotten example of the tastes and textures Gouffé indicated. The results are almost Asian in their minimalism. Once emptied of its vegetables, the dish's spiced acidic oil provides a perfect marinade for sardines, or anchovies, or even store-bought pickles, and a good poaching liquid for clams or oysters.

In his fine *Dictionnaire de l'Art Culinaire Français,* Manfred Höfler gives vegetables *à la grecque* a first date in print, by Escoffier, of 1894. Escoffier himself writes that he witnessed Greek cooks prepare vegetables this way. Others dispute that Greeks ever cooked it, crediting the designation *à la grecque* instead to the dish's having arrived in France with migrants from the Ottoman empire. Whatever these piquant, oily delights are called—and for whatever reason—they are not Greek at all, but as French as the fat luscious snail and bouillabaisse.

I make mine with many kinds of mushrooms and a good deal more olive oil and herbs than the long-departed male *cuisiniers* did. I include brown sugar, which has a wonderful effect but is neither Ottoman nor French. I think they are ambrosial.

VEGETABLES À LA GRECQUE

1 cup good olive oil
½ cup white wine vinegar
¼ cup red wine vinegar
¼ cup good white wine
4 cups water
5½ teaspoons salt
1 tablespoon coriander seeds
1 tablespoon fennel seeds
1 tablespoon brown sugar
2 whole dried chiles
2 whole bay leaves
1 teaspoon saffron threads
a few whole sprigs fresh thyme
1 medium onion, halved vertically, then sliced vertically
2 cups thinly, vertically cut fennel
6 cups quartered flavorful mushrooms (separated by type) or
        cauliflower
2 cups thinly, diagonally cut celery

Combine the liquids and spices and herbs in a pot and bring to just below a boil. Cook each vegetable in the seasoned liquid, separated by type. Start with the onions, then the fennel, then the mushrooms, then the celery. Cook each until it can be pierced with a knife and tastes delicious. As each one is done, scoop it out with a slotted spoon or handheld sieve onto a cookie sheet to cool.

If spices or bits of herb get stuck to the vegetable, put what you can back into the pot, and don't worry about the rest—everything will marinate together and things will redistribute. When all the vegetables are cooked, layer them into jars—it looks nice if you start with mushrooms, continue with onions, etc. Pour the cooking liquid over them, without straining it. The olive oil in the liquid will rise to the top and create a seal. Refrigerate for up to a month.

From here, you can do what you like, exchanging any vegetable but the nightshades for mushrooms or cauliflower and following M. Gouffé's discreet footsteps.

Serve these just warm enough for their lovely oily dressing to be liquid, in a pretty shallow bowl with small forks and a lot of good bread. Richard Olney observed that vegetables *à la grecque* are "not of a nature to flatter a wine." I supply my own blunter recommendation: they are best accompanied by gin.

Another vegetable that benefits from hors d'œuvre pickling but demands a different treatment is the eggplant. I have a recipe for *aubergines en hors d'œuvre* from Escoffier's last student Joseph Donon's *The Classic French Cuisine*, which provides a spiritual if not technical model for my method. My technique is probably older, closer to Italian *melanzane sott'aceto* or the Persian pickled eggplant that an assiduous Persian cook tells me is as old as Rudaki.

AUBERGINES EN HORS D'ŒUVRE

Note: The eggplants to do this with are the little Fairy Tale ones. If those aren't around, cut what you have into strange little pieces, about the size of two thumbs, and use a little less salt.

1 pound very small, beautiful eggplants
3 cloves garlic, unpeeled
1 or 2 not terribly spicy fresh (or dried) chiles, split down the
     middle
⅛ teaspoon whole fresh (or dried) coriander seeds

1 tablespoon kosher salt
½ cup olive oil
¼ cup water
¼ cup white wine
¼ cup red wine vinegar
whole sprigs thyme
whole sprigs rosemary
2 bay leaves

Heat the oven to 375 degrees. Put everything in a shallow heavy oven-safe pot big enough to hold it in nearly a single layer. Cook, covered, for about 35 minutes, until the eggplant is quite tender. Turn the oven temperature up to 400 degrees and uncover. Cook for about 25 minutes more, until much of the liquid is gone and the eggplant has just begun to sink and brown. Remove from the oven. Allow to cool. Serve at room temperature.

After having been eaten alongside gin cocktails, vegetables *à la grecque* and *aubergines en hors d'œuvre* can be put back into the oil and vinegar in which they were cooked and eaten the next day, and the following one. They make of a humble sandwich—whether of French ham, Chinese tofu, or Italian mozzarella—a great one.

A quaint and amusing way of serving pickled things is impaled on toothpicks. This is done in Basque country, where one finds several elements of M. Gouffé's old list on a single wooden spear: pickles, oil-marinated anchovies, and fat green olives.

Such stacks are elegant with vegetables *à la grecque* or *aubergines en hors d'œuvres*. I make them most often like the Basques, who christened their traditional trinity of pickled peppers, anchovy, and olive with the pretty name "Gilda." These are especially cunning because, being composed of ingredients entirely from tins and jars, they are as easy to serve midwinter as mid-May.

GILDAS

1 jar pitted Spanish green olives
1 can best-possible big anchovies—ideally Spanish, because they
    are especially rosy and fat
1 jar pickled guindilla peppers, found in specialty or Spanish
    stores
toothpicks

Onto each toothpick, put 1 olive, then the end of 1 anchovy, leaving the rest dangling. Then 2 guindilla peppers, horizontally. Then pierce the other end of the anchovy so the fish embraces the peppers, and finally add another olive.

With gildas in mind, you can, if you want, add a cornichon, or a whole little tomato preserved in oil, or smoked mussels, or replace anchovies—which you don't like—with cocktail onions—which you do, both in your Gibson and on your plate.

The category of pickle is most odd-shaped and insubordinate, which I mention to introduce its most symmetrical member: the pickled egg.

I am tempted to further editorialize and write "the ignominious pickled egg." The worst of these, as any frequent driver cross-country knows, marinate in some cross between sulfur, formaldehyde, and floor cleaner. If you have ever sat before such pickled eggs, bobbing in their infernal primordial stew, at a counter outside Tallahassee, you will have wondered what came over whomever crammed the first innocent hundred or so into a large jar, settled it for all time atop the Platonic bar, and called the result edible.

The answer is, a will to survive. Before refrigeration, eggs—which stay good unwashed and unwatched on a counter for several weeks—had to keep longer. They were sometimes dipped into paraffin. In a better-tasting arrangement, housewives applied the preservative power of vinegar and pickling spices to the harvest of the henhouse. Now that we have such good refrigeration, pickled eggs don't need to be as inviolate to injury, destruction, and decay. They can be subtler and less eternal.

Here is a recipe for pickled eggs that are not rubbery, acid, and abstract. The eggs are softly cooked and the vinegar administered judiciously. I advise only making these when both eggs and garlic are full and fresh—fresh spring or summer garlic is vital. They will not last on bars for any longer than your drink.

PICKLED EGGS

4 eggs
1 large clove fresh uncured summer garlic
½ teaspoon sea salt
¼ cup white wine vinegar
optional: a few leaves fresh parsley or basil, or celery leaves

Boil eggs by not boiling them: put the eggs in a pot and fill with cold water to cover. Bring the water to a boil, covered, then shut off the heat and wait 5 to 6 minutes, depending on the size of your eggs. Run under cold water or dunk in ice water. Peel.

Slice the garlic and mix with the salt and vinegar in a jar. Leave for 10 minutes. Once the eggs are cool, combine them with the garlic vinegar in the jar and set in the refrigerator, lightly rotating it every now and again. Let sit for at least a few hours and up to overnight to let the eggs become vinegared.

An hour or 2 before serving, remove the eggs, slice them in half lengthwise, salt the yolks, then pour the pickling liquid over them equally. Dot the egg halves with herbs, if using. Serve at cool room temperature.

A friend gave me a milk-glass plate with scalloped edges and egg-shaped indentations of the sort one used to bring to church buffets. It is a slightly eerie hue of sea-foam green, and I like it. I put my pickled eggs in its shallow wells until my husband, who finds the color and perhaps the concept unsettling, spies the offense and moves them to a plainer plate. I surrender in the interest of domestic peace, and because the serene white-and-marigold halves look dignified anywhere, including on Basque toothpicks, perhaps with a judicious pickled pepper between the two.

A particularly lovely version of these can be made with pullet eggs—from birds as small and tender as the eggs they lay—or quail eggs. In either case, the only change is egg cooking time: 3 to 4 minutes for pullet, 2 to 3 for quail.

The deviled egg has endured more keenly than any food of its era, save (and *Hail!*) the Caesar salad. In its archetypical form—hard-boiled eggs, yolks removed and mixed with cayenne, mustard, and purchased mayonnaise, piped decoratively into waiting whites—it is basically good. Despite often being made with poor-quality eggs, that primitive version survives because it offers the likable contrast of a luxurious filling in a monkish frame.

To make my deviled eggs—which are really a step backward, not forward—one must not-boil eggs—that is: follow the instructions for cooking eggs on page 14—then, once they are cooked and peeled, mix the yolks with homemade mayonnaise made of 1 egg yolk to 1 cup olive oil, a dab of Dijon mustard, and a good squeeze of lemon. That rough mixture should be spooned back into waiting egg whites, which will not have become leathery, because they have not been jostled. There you have my slightly barbaric deviled eggs, especially if there are chives or their blossoms or some small wild cress to scatter into a rustic field over them.

There exists an even older version of the deviled egg. It was invented—if a word implying inquiry and revelation can be sanely applied—by a seventeenth-century French chef with the musical name Pierre de Lune, which he (or we) bestowed upon his stuffed eggs, calling them *oeufs Pierre de Lune*. M. de Lune's eggs were a dramatic spiced affair, combining sweet cream steeped with a bouquet of scallion, thyme, and cloves; cooked yolks; a chlorophyllic fillip of blanched small lettuces, sorrel, spinach, chervil, parsley; and a single, inscrutable mushroom.

Here is a version I concocted with a warm-faced cook named Samin Nosrat, which is faster and, I think, better. They are a fine and classic addition to a church buffet, and delicious in more secular settings.

EGGS PIERRE DE LUNE–NOSRAT

8 eggs
2 cloves garlic
¼ teaspoon kosher salt, plus a tiny bit for garlic
6 anchovies fillets

⅓ cup grated Parmesan cheese
¼ cup olive oil
juice of ½ lemon
1 teaspoon white wine vinegar
freshly ground black pepper
3 leaves romaine lettuce, very thinly sliced

Follow the instructions for cooking eggs on page 14. Peel and halve them, vertically, and scoop the yolks into a bowl.

Roughly chop the garlic and smash it to a paste with a small pinch of salt in a mortar or on a cutting board. Finely chop the anchovies and mix well with the garlic. Add to the yolks along with the Parmesan, olive oil, lemon juice, and vinegar. Add the salt and freshly ground black pepper, and mix. Taste and adjust. Add the romaine, mix well, and using a small spoon, fill the waiting egg whites with the mixture. These can be chilled for a few hours. Bring to room temperature for 15 minutes before serving.

Whereas the smaller the egg, the more elegant the pickled egg, eggs Pierre de Lune–Nosrat reach their pinnacle when made with duck eggs, which tend to be larger, deeper hued, and even more faultlessly lunar.

If you have only two eggs and an hors d'œuvres table to furnish— or if you overcooked eggs you'd planned to devil or de Lune, make an egg pâté. This is particularly good economy if made from botched eggs *and* cheese ends, optimistically wrapped in wax paper some time ago, lingering in the back of your cheese drawer. You can also use any good, gratable cheddar. This is a wonderful spread for dark toast or crackers or crisp vegetables.

PÂTÉ D'OEUF

¼ cup grated sweet onions and/or finely sliced scallions
a squeeze of fresh lemon juice
kosher salt and freshly ground black pepper
4 ounces good cheddar cheese, like Cabot Extra Sharp or Cabot

Clothbound, or bits and bobs of any sharp, gratable cheese
but blue, grated
2 eggs, boiled and mashed
2 tablespoons mayonnaise
1 tablespoon olive oil

Soak the onions in a squeeze of lemon juice with a pinch of salt for 10 minutes. Add the rest of the ingredients. Taste for salt and adjust.

The word *pâté* can make today's cook wary, possessing the triple features of being French, suggesting offal (that stigmatized animal part that is not muscle, but *other*), and having indefinite boundary— where, after all, does "terrine" end and "pâté" begin? And what of the foundational fact that *pâté* means "paste," and whether it's almond paste for marzipan or pork liver depends entirely on context?

As with other dishes that proliferated during last century's adulation of *la cuisine française*, some pâtés are fussy and intimidating; some are not. Those that are *not* share traits that are a boon to any home cook: consisting mostly of inexpensive ingredients and parts or pieces often discarded, and making of a molehill of odds and ends a mountain (or pretty pâté) of coherent allure.

Pigs' livers are hefty things that were the basis of most pâtés of the Francophilic era. Chicken livers, on the other hand, are small and manageable, and pâtés of them quite doable in one's own kitchen.

A good number of chicken liver pâtés appear on restaurant menus now—on *most*, even, of a certain breed. But a majority seem overcooked and *boozy*, as though, worried about the carnality of pâté's main ingredient their makers invoke a spirit to quell it. This chicken liver pâté recipe was given to me by my brother, a chef with a taste for neglected old ways that matches mine and skill for resuscitating them that exceeds it.

CHICKEN LIVER À LA TOSCANE

1 pound chicken livers, any little membranes or connective
tissue pared

kosher salt
⅓ cup good olive oil, plus a little more
1 cup dry vermouth, divided
2 cups minced white or yellow onion
3 cloves garlic, finely minced
3 tablespoons best pickled capers or, better yet, salted capers,
    soaked and rinsed several times
9 anchovy fillets
2 tablespoons chopped fresh rosemary
2 tablespoons chopped fresh sage
⅔ to 1 cup crème fraîche

Season the livers with salt. In a very hot pan, in one or two batches, sear the livers in a single layer in just enough olive oil to keep them from sticking, until cooked to medium-rare, about 1½ minutes on the first side and 10 to 20 seconds on the second. They splatter terribly, so be prepared to duck or use a screen over the pan. Deglaze the pan with ⅓ cup vermouth after each batch and pour over cooked livers on a plate. Cool.

*   Cook the onion with ½ teaspoon salt in the olive oil over medium heat until tender, then add the garlic and cook together until barely caramelized. Add the capers. Cook until they begin to toast. Add the anchovies and cook until they melt completely, and everything takes on a sticky appearance. Add the herbs, then the remaining vermouth, scraping with a wooden spoon to deglaze. Cook until the wine smell is gone. Cool.*

*   Combine the livers, including any liquid that has collected around them, and the crème fraîche in a food processor and purée until completely smooth. Add the onion, garlic, caper, anchovy, herb mixture and pulse to a texture you like, leaving it a bit rough, if that pleases you, as it does me.*

I made this pâté for my brother's wedding, and in the thin, hardly remembered hours of the night we spread it recklessly on cold fried chicken, an unintentional symbol of continuity and closed loops. It is also good spread onto radishes or on little crisp toasts. After hors d'œuvre hour ends, it makes wonderful sandwiches, spread very cold and thick onto baguettes adorned otherwise with lightly dressed lettuces and onion or cucumber pickles.

The first time I read the words *shrimp pâté*, I fell into a sort of culinary trance. It was in M.F.K. Fisher's *How to Cook a Wolf*, and I loved it, though its ingredients were crude: canned shrimp, raw onion, bought mayonnaise.

Here is a version that is a mix between M.F.K. Fisher's, the shrimp pâtés made today in our own Lowcountry, and a prawn paste from Elizabeth David's 1970 *Spices, Salt and Aromatics in the English Kitchen*. While made of a rare and expensive ingredient—wild shrimp—the pâté is still economical: the shells can be kept and turned into shrimp stock (see page 60), which is gratifying for whoever has paid the shrimp-man, and a pound of shrimp makes enough pâté for a party.

SHRIMP PÂTÉ

1 pound large shell-on wild shrimp
½ cup olive oil
kosher salt
3 to 4 tablespoons dry sherry, plus to taste
1 large shallot, diced (about 3 heaping tablespoons)
1 clove garlic, pounded to a paste with a pinch of salt
a good deal of fresh lemon juice
a lot of freshly ground black pepper

Peel and devein the shrimp. Freeze the shells to turn into shrimp stock—or make stock now and freeze it. Heat a large pan and add 2 tablespoons of the olive oil, then the shrimp, and salt them lightly. Cook for about a minute on each side until the shrimp are pink and just firm. Remove to a plate to cool, adding sherry to deglaze the pan. Pour the deglazing liquid over the cooling shrimp. Heat the pan again. Add 2 tablespoons of the olive oil, then the shallot, and salt it lightly. Cook over medium heat until translucent, then add the garlic. Cook until both are easily broken with a wooden spoon but not brown. Transfer the shallot mixture to the bowl of a food processor. Add the shrimp, a squeeze of lemon juice, and another drizzle of sherry. Pulse to combine, adding the remaining olive oil slowly as you do. Once integrated, taste. Adjust salt, lemon juice, and sherry, then add black pepper. Let rest several hours, refrigerated, for the flavors to meld. Refrigerate for up to 2 days if not serving immediately, pressing plastic wrap directly against the pâté's surface to prevent oxidation. Remove from the refrigerator 15 minutes before serving with white toast, saltine crackers, or potato chips.

Pounded coriander seeds, fresh or dried, can be added to the mixture; lime juice can replace lemon, as in Elizabeth David's prawn paste. Any herb, as long as it is still fresh and green, can be chopped and sprinkled over at the end.

A strange and delicious thing to do with any leftover pâté is to spread it thickly on cold white bread, press sesame seeds over the top, chill it further, and fry the bread, in its entirety, in several inches of very hot peanut oil. I have copied this procedure from Gabrielle Hamilton at Prune, who I believe copied it from the Hong Kongese, who serve shrimp toast as dim sum, or perhaps an afternoon snack. Leftover pâté is also miraculous stirred into hot polenta or risotto or congee or grits.

As with pickled eggs and pâté, refrigeration has mostly obviated the *need* to pickle seafood, opening the door to pickling it purely for pleasure. To the uninitiated, pickled shrimp, a stalwart of the 1940s-to-1960s American buffet, probably sounds horrid. But when made with lavish amounts of lemon juice and olive oil and a restrained hand with vinegar, they are a revelation. Elegant, but with a ruddy air, pickled shrimp must be one of the finest warm-weather hors d'œuvres. This version closely follows Frank Stitt's in *Frank Stitt's Southern Table.*

PICKLED SHRIMP

1 teaspoon black peppercorns
4 bay leaves
onion skin, leek top, or a quarter of an onion
3 cloves garlic: 1 left whole, 2 thinly sliced lengthwise

bouquet garni of parsley stems and a few sprigs thyme, if you
    have them
2 teaspoons kosher salt, plus to taste
2 pounds peeled and deveined shrimp, tails on
4 scallions or spring onions, thinly sliced lengthwise
½ cup fresh lemon juice
¼ cup white wine vinegar
1½ teaspoons fennel seeds
1½ teaspoons coriander seeds
5 to 10 dried árbol chiles, broken once or left whole
1 lemon, quartered, seeded, and thinly sliced
1 cup olive oil
optional: a big handful chopped fresh parsley or oregano

Make poaching liquid for the shrimp: Put the peppercorns, bay leaves, onion skin, whole garlic clove, and bouquet garni in a big pot of water. Bring to a boil, then reduce the heat and let simmer for 10 minutes. Add 1 teaspoon salt and the shrimp. Turn off the heat and let stand for 2 to 3 minutes to poach the shrimp. Remove the shrimp with a strainer to a tray. Do not refrigerate. Save the broth for soup and keep the bay leaves.

    In a separate bowl, combine the scallions, lemon juice, vinegar, fennel and coriander seeds, chiles, lemon, and sliced garlic. Add the bay leaves. Let sit for 5 minutes. Add the shrimp and mix, then add the olive oil and mix. Refrigerate, covering once cool, at least 5 hours and ideally overnight. Bring to room temperature for 10 to 15 minutes before serving. Add the fresh herbs, if using, at the last possible moment.

These are *good* a few hours after they're made, but *doggedly good* the next day.

Once you are comfortable with the basic formula, you can apply it to other sea-things. An especially good alternative are mussels. (There is a recipe on page 62 for an old-fashioned creamy mussel soup called *potage Billy By* that is made of mussels, but served without them, leaving two pounds of perfectly cooked and seasoned mussels naked and shivering and in need of a home.) You might also use clams, white fish cut into pieces, little sweet scallops. Any version appreciates saltines or crisp toasts for soaking up its juices.

It is only upon considering together the hors d'œuvres of earlier days that one sees how many of our eating habits and the fashion for one or another have revolved around the absence, pursuit, and possession of means to keep food from "spoiling." Aspics and forms and molds and shapes—as various jelled dishes that came into vogue in the nineteenth century were called—were at first a form of boasting that one possessed an icebox or a great allowance to spend on ice, as jells do not jell unless they are chilled.

All are among the more clinically correct foods one can serve, possessing a smooth, transparent, almost machine-like form. Our view of such perfection has dimmed. Today, an aspic must *taste good*, as well as appear that way. When such an anachronism does taste good, however, it is surprising and refreshing.

My introduction to tomato aspic, a mainstay of tables *haute* and *bas* in midcentury America, came, oddly, in Italy, in a low white building with its old-fashioned gold sign reading *Cibreo*. I nodded timidly at the waiter's recitations without knowing to what strange course I had submitted myself. Its start was tomato aspic, under the Italian name *gelatina di pomodoro:* a bright red upturned half globe, served with small silver spoons. It was cool but full of the warm tastes of olive oil and summer tomatoes. I knew I had encountered something ageless and good.

This produces something very like Cibreo's.

GELATINA DI POMODORO

1½ to 2 pounds best summer tomatoes (as to variety, Ed Behr,
    of *The Art of Eating*, recommends the Cosmonaut Volkov [!]
    for cooking. If you can find the Cosmonaut, choose him/
    it. In the winter, very sweet cherry tomatoes can stand in.)
1 envelope (¼ ounce), plus a little bit from a second, unflavored
    powdered gelatin
3 tablespoons finely julienned basil, cut just before using
1 small clove garlic, smashed to a fine paste with a tiny bit of salt
1 small fresh chile, finely minced
2 teaspoons kosher salt
3 tablespoons best olive oil, plus more for drizzling

Halve the tomatoes if they are not cherry. If you mind seeds, squeeze over a fine-mesh sieve set over a bowl to remove them, reserving all the juice. Seeded or not, purée the tomatoes until smooth, passing the purée through a food mill if you have one. Otherwise simply continue. Add the reserved juice to make a total of 2¼ cups tomato pulp. Transfer ½ cup to a wide small bowl, sprinkle the gelatin over, stir, and let hydrate for 3 minutes. Heat the remaining in a small pot until boiling, add the softened gelatin mixture, and stir well to dissolve the gelatin, then add the basil, garlic, chile, salt, and olive oil and turn off the heat. Lightly oil a 1-quart mold, or 4 to 6 individual ones. Pour the aspic into the mold(s) and refrigerate for at least 3 hours, until set. To unmold, run a knife between the aspic and the mold. Unmold the aspic onto a plate. Drizzle with olive oil and serve cold, with spoons.

Little toasts for scooping the *gelatina* are pleasant. A cool, halved soft-cooked egg alongside can also be very nice, as can, if you are in the spirit of strange, wobbly textures, a dollop of homemade mayonnaise (page 171).

To echo M.F.K. Fisher: "This is not that, and that is certainly not this," and an egg suspended in aspic has as little to do with what I ate a decade ago in a Florentine dining room as it does with a boiled egg. But an *oeuf en gelée* is an aspic, as it is a boiled egg. It is moreover a boiled egg suspended like a jewel in jelled strong broth the interior of which appears to have been strung with tiny leaves of herb, thumbnail-sized golden tomatoes, filaments of sweet chile, edible flowers.

Oeufs en gelée are a pleasure to gaze at, and a greater pleasure to eat. They are easy to make if you have good-tasting broth or consommé on hand, and a pain if you must start with bird carcasses and water. If you have good broth, it is worth the small trouble, to watch the happiness on your guests' faces as yolks spill into the jelled soup and strong herbs about them.

OEUFS EN GELÉE

Note: A "raft" is used to clarify stock here. If you don't mind some lingering muddiness, ignore all directions concerning it. If you are curious about clarifying, try it once. The entire process consists of dumping an unappealing mixture into soup and watching it do the unexpected.

a few black peppercorns, lightly crushed
6 sprigs parsley, chopped
3 egg whites and eggshells—make sure no yolk interferes
¼ cup ground turkey
½ leek or 3 scallions, chopped and well washed
½ carrot, chopped
4 cups good chicken broth
2 to 3 tablespoons dry sherry
kosher salt

½ cup cold water

just barely under 2 envelopes (½ ounce) unflavored powdered
    gelatin

canola oil, for greasing

an assortment of pretty, fragrant small herb leaves and garnishes,
    like piccolo fino basil, chervil, fresh green coriander seeds,
    tiny tomatoes, slices of vegetables *à la grecque* (page 10)

6 boiled eggs, cooked according to the directions on page 14 but
    left only 4½ to 5 minutes, and peeled

*Pulse the peppercorns, parsley sprigs, egg whites and eggshells, turkey,
leek, and carrot briefly in a food processor to combine. This is the raft.
Combine the broth and raft ingredients in a small saucepan. Bring to a
slow boil over medium heat, stirring, until the egg whites start to gather
into a soft crust, 7 to 10 minutes. Simmer over low heat without stirring
for 20 minutes.*

*Set a fine-mesh sieve lined with a coffee filter or double layer of
cheesecloth over a bowl. Using a ladle, make a hole in the raft and ladle
the broth out through the hole into the bowl. Add sherry to taste. Season
very well with salt—more than you're inclined. Put the cold water in a
small very wide bowl and sprinkle the gelatin over; let stand for 3 minutes, until it has hydrated and swelled. Add the gelatin mixture to the hot
broth and stir well to dissolve. Refrigerate the bowl for 5 to 10 minutes
until the broth is cool but not set.*

*Lightly grease four small ramekins or bowls with canola oil. Pour
a few scant teaspoons of aspic into each. Chill until almost set, 10 to 20
minutes. Make a pretty design of your garnishes in the aspic. (The bottom of the mold will be the top of the unmolded oeuf.) Top each with 1
tablespoon of the aspic. Chill again until set. Place 1 boiled egg in each
mold, surround with more garnishes. Cover with the remaining aspic,
dividing it evenly. Chill until completely set, about 3 to 4 hours. To serve,
run a knife around the insides of the ramekins, dip the bottoms in a bowl
of warm water for 5 seconds, then invert onto plates. Serve with a bright
salad and toasted or grilled bread.*

These make a substantial and somewhat pretentious first course.
They are best served when you are able to drink wine in an unem-

barrassed way, and followed with a rich sturdy workhorse like pot-roasted chicken or beef. Or with the horse itself—the best successor I've ever had to an *oeuf en gelée* was at a dark restaurant in Montreal so full of epicurism and festivity it was really impossible to see: a thick, bloodred filet of horse, sauced with truffles and foie gras, with fried potatoes on the side.

"There is more simplicity," wrote G. K. Chesterton, "in the man who eats caviar on impulse than in the man who eats grapefruit on principle." I keep this small wisdom about me, finding it a guiding light through a number of behavioral thickets.

But what would Chesterton have made of caviar by design? An icy tin of salty fish eggs can be bought on a whim, opened with a pocketknife, and eaten with soda crackers, but a caviar *pie* must be plotted and planned.

Caviar pie, which is today unknown, was popular in the late 1970s and grew more so in the 1980s. Craig Claiborne wrote a 1978 column in the *New York Times* called "Luxurious Leftovers," which began, "Blessed, indeed, is the house that finds itself on this first day of the year with some leftover caviar in the refrigerator . . . we offer a relatively inexpensive red caviar pie."

But the dish is a good deal older. Bartolomeo Scappi served caviar pie at a banquet for the Holy Roman Emperor Charles V. I can't find what Scappi's included. Craig Claiborne's contained sour cream, hard-boiled egg, and onion, formed into a "pie" and topped with caviar. (It is kitschy but not altogether bad.)

This version, more *pot de crème* than pie, possesses a slightly affected suavity. It was taught to me by my brother.

CAVIAR-LEEK POTS DE CRÈME

4 cups sliced leeks, white and light green parts only, well washed
2 tablespoons water
1 tablespoon kosher salt, plus to taste
2 cups heavy cream
½ bunch chives, finely chopped

olive oil
1 envelope (¼ ounce) unflavored powdered gelatin per 2 cups
    leek purée
canola oil for greasing
1 ounce paddlefish caviar or other good caviar

Sweat the leeks in the water and salt in a covered saucepot until mostly covered by water and the liquid they release. Add the cream and simmer, uncovered, until the leeks are completely tender when pierced with a sharp knife. Make chive pistou by pounding chives with a tiny sprinkle of salt in a mortar or on a cutting board, then adding just enough olive oil to make a spoonable oily paste. Purée the leek-cream mixture in a blender (be careful, as it will be hot). Strain through a fine-mesh sieve or chinoise set over a bowl. Measure and transfer to a clean pot. Season with salt. Add gelatin, according to your quantity of leek purée. Turn off the heat and pour into 8 oiled individual ramekins or small bowls or demi-tasse cups or a springform pan; swirl or dollop ½ teaspoon chive pistou into each. Chill for at least 3 hours and up to overnight. Remove from the refrigerator a few minutes before serving. Release from the springform pan or serve directly in the ramekins. Top thickly with caviar, and serve, with a crisp toast or two, or crackers, alongside each.

These little *pots de crème* are best served as a chaste course all their own. If they look too austere, there is also some logic to serving a bowl of boiled potatoes, instead of crackers, onto which the delicate pudding might be scooped and spread. As to what to serve after, why not chicken à la Montmorency (page 166) or scrambled eggs with chanterelles, and a bowl of good ripe fruit or shortbread?

There is no hot hors d'œuvre I prefer to a roasted oyster, its frail edges white-hot, its pale silver muscle warm and flushed, dabbed with fast-melting sweet butter, perhaps an herb or speck of sweet onion, a single drop of pepper sauce . . .

I cannot say exactly when or where roasted oysters were first eaten. According to the little book *Oyster: A Gastronomic History*, by Drew Smith, oysters predated us, and whatever day some forgotten ancestor tipped a basket into a fire, making a favorable gastronomic slip, passed without official record. The first *recipe* for roast oysters was surely only spoken and sounded like a taciturn: *Throw 'em in now, and take 'em out when they're hot!* I have read dozens of oyster recipes, most good, but I think this by Marion Harland from 1871 is the best:

Roast Oysters

There is no pleasanter frolic for an Autumn evening, in the regions where oysters are plentiful, than an impromptu "roast" in the kitchen. There the oysters are hastily thrown into the fire by the peck. You may consider that your fastidious taste is marvelously respected if they are washed first. A bushel basket is set to receive the empty shells, and the click of the oyster-knives forms a constant accompaniment to the music of laughing voices. Nor are roast oysters amiss upon your own quiet supper-table, when the "good man" comes in on a wet night, tired and hungry, and wants "something heartening." Wash and wipe the shell-oysters, and lay them in the oven, if it is quick; upon the top of the stove, if it is not. When they open, they are done. Pile in a large dish and send to table. Remove the upper shell by a dexterous wrench of the knife, season the oyster on the lower, with pepper-sauce and butter, or pepper, salt, and vinegar in lieu of the sauce, and you have the very aroma of this pearl of bivalves, pure and undefiled. Or, you may open while raw, leaving the oysters upon the lower shells; lay in a large baking-pan, and roast in their own liquor, adding pepper, salt, and butter before serving.

Ah, me, as they used to say, how her recipe makes me long for the pure tastes it invokes.

Here is another recipe, lacking Mrs. Harland's fireside clicks, but including present-day conventions such as oven temperature and measurements. It produces, nonetheless, as undefiled a dish. You may need a knife to coax apart the shells, but they shouldn't require "a dexterous wrench."

ROAST OYSTERS WITH PEPPER SAUCE

2 dozen good small oysters
4 tablespoons (½ stick) unsalted butter
Tabasco or other vinegary hot pepper sauce

Set the oven to broil. Put a heavy baking sheet on the top rack, as close to the heat source as possible. Scrub the oysters well under fast-running water. Divide the butter into 24 little cubes or just leave the stick at room temperature to take dabs off without measuring.

When the broiler is hot, make sure the butter, Tabasco, and guests are nearby, then spread as many oysters on the hot baking sheet as fit in a single layer. Broil until they gasp open—under a minute. Remove and dab butter and a drop of Tabasco in each opened oyster. Return to the oven a moment longer, then remove and lift the top shells off the buttered and sauced oysters by hand or with an oyster knife. (Butter and sauce any that didn't open the first time now, and after removing all the finished ones, return those to the oven for an instant before shucking.) These are best served directly to whomever is closest to the oven. If you find that too informal, put those that are ready to be eaten on a plate and urge guests to eat directly from it, as you turn to the next round.

Even better is if you find yourself with the modern convenience of culinary calculations and the primeval luxury of live fire. Cooked on a grate over hot coals, roast oysters are more delicious yet. Or maybe you are just hungrier.

If you are so lucky, follow the same instructions (see above), making sure the oysters' ridged shells are set too high for flames to lick. A large rosy steak, seasoned with salt and sprigs of rosemary, can be placed upon the grate the instant the last of the oysters has hissed and sizzled. This, next to small potatoes that have been wrapped in foil and cooked in the fire's embers, topped liberally with butter, may be the best collaboration yet between human and natural designs. But then again, if you can find more oysters and more wood, why not instead add oysters to roast until both you and your supply are exhausted?

There are many things besides butter and hot sauce you can put in an oyster and roast it. Maître d'hôtel butter makes a fine coat for a chilly bivalve; a little dab of the Sicilian tomato condiment called *estratto* with or without a shard of guanciale or pancetta laid upon it is a happy marriage of land and sea. Oysters Rockefeller, which can be the most pleasant, used to be the most common, having been made famous, probably justly, by travelers to Antoine's, in New Orleans, who tasted the dish made by the sure hand of its inventor, Jules Alciatore, in 1899. What was *in* his version, no one knows—I have read of a laboratory analysis of an oyster Rockefeller from present-day Antoine's that concluded that it contains the anise-flavored spirit Herbsaint and no spinach. This lasting mystery leaves a cook free to experiment, blissfully unburdened with duty to fealty.

Here is a version that is truly delicious and, I flatter myself to think, as deserving of the surname Rockefeller as whatever secret combination Mr. Alciatore took to his grave. As John Thorne wrote of the oysters Rockefeller recipe in his somewhat strangely named *Serious Pig*, "It's still a dressing that knows you came to eat the surf, not the turf."

OYSTERS ROCKEFELLER

1 dozen good oysters
rock salt or other coarse salt
bottled clam juice (buy 2 bottles, though you may only use 1)
4 tablespoons (½ stick) unsalted butter
1 or 2 stalks celery, minced (about ⅓ cup)
4 or 5 scallions, minced (about ⅓ cup)
¼ cup all-purpose flour
1 cup mixed fresh soft herbs (tarragon, celery leaf, parsley,
    savory, chervil, etc.)
3 tablespoons grated stale bread or fresh breadcrumbs

Scrub the oysters well under fast-running water. Shuck over a pan or plate, pouring all the liquid they release into a measuring cup through a fine-mesh strainer. Release the oysters from their bottom shells. Cover a rimmed baking sheet with rock salt and nestle the oysters in the salt to steady them. Add clam juice to the oyster liquid in the measuring cup to make 1⅓ cups liquid.

Melt the butter in a little pot. Add the celery and scallions. Cook for a minute over very low heat. Add the flour, whisking to keep it from browning. Slowly add the oyster liquid mixture, whisking the whole time. Bring to a boil for an instant as you whisk. Turn the burner to the lowest possible setting and cook, whisking occasionally, for 20 minutes, or until the velouté doesn't taste floury. Add the herbs. Cool for several minutes. Blend in a blender until smooth.

Set the oven to broil. Spoon a teaspoon of the herb velouté into each oyster. Top lightly with breadcrumbs. Broil until browned, 4 to 6 minutes. Serve quickly.

After such a heady beginning, something sophisticated but brawny is best. Perhaps chicken cooked in leftover wine (page 164), or steak haché (page 182), or a vigorous mound of steak tartare (page 180), which will make you feel strong.

If you are wondering, as the editor of these pages did, why anyone would want to cook an oyster, plain, filled, or any way at all, perhaps a glimmer of logic comes from Voltaire, who wrote: "I feel there is something barbarous in eating such a pretty little animal raw."

Generations before ours ate more clams—as pretty and safely eaten raw and cooked—than we do. *Why* is hard to settle. I can guess— and do—that clams' shells seem an inconvenience now that progress has delivered meals already made. The other reason I can think of is that clams are resolutely workingman's food. They are available, as they ever were, on a workingman's salary. Clams can't be eaten for prestige, which might, in certain circles, darken their allure.

If you reject those views, there is occasional sense to making clams Casino and serving them as they were served at the Casino restaurant in Narragansett, Rhode Island. They were invented there by Julius Keller, the seaside restaurant's maître d', whom I imagine serving them on a great platter, with a carafe of light cool Italian wine, followed by some sort of odorously grilled chop and a tomato and lettuce salad.

Our most diligent culinary scholars have been foiled searching for Keller's exact formula, as for Jules Alciatore's. James Beard wrote that it was "certain that green peppers and bacon are two of the origi- nal ingredients . . . the others remain a mystery." There are proba- bly as many different ways to interpret and clarify that mystery as there are cooks to try. My own way is a partial insurrection. I have resolved by experiment that green pepper is overly assertive, and the smallest allowance mutes even the strongest-voiced clam. I favor more community-minded fennel and leek. Brightly herbal and only tri- flingly adorned with bacon, these have a clear precision.

CLAMS CASINO

24 cherrystone or littleneck clams
½ cup diced fennel bulb or stalk
½ cup sliced leeks or chopped yellow onion
2 cloves garlic, unpeeled
3 or 4 hot chiles, halved
olive oil

⅔ cup white wine
2 tablespoons diced bacon
6 tablespoons chopped mixed fresh herbs (celery leaf, parsley,
     oregano, savory, fennel fronds)
1 tablespoon heavy cream
lemon wedges, for serving

*Scrub the clams well under fast-running water. In a heavy pot, cook
the fennel, leeks, garlic, and chiles in a few tablespoons of olive oil until
softened, 2 to 3 minutes. Add the clams and wine and cook, covered, over
high heat until the clams gasp open. Remove them as they do. There will
be stragglers. Let them cook until they open. Discard any that, after 7
minutes, do not.*

Strain the broth through a fine-mesh sieve into a bowl.

*Remove the clams from their shells and roughly chop, adding any
liquid they emit to the strained broth. Wash half of the clamshells and
leave to dry.*

*Cook the bacon over low heat in the empty pot. Remove some of the
fat if it's very fatty bacon. Add the clam broth and cook until reduced
to ⅓ to ⅔ cup. Remove to a bowl. Add the herbs, cream, and clams and
combine.*

*Set the oven to broil. Fill the clean clamshells abundantly with the
clam mixture. Arrange in a single layer in roasting pans. Cook under
the broiler until bubbling and lightly browned, about 5 minutes. Serve
immediately, with lemon and spoons.*

I serve clams Casino alongside crisp toast rubbed with a halved
garlic clove and a very ripe tomato, doused with olive oil—a barefaced
imitation of the Spanish *pan con tomate*—and accompanied by crisp
Italian white wine or beer.

You might also treat clams more delicately, steaming them open
without chiles, and then reducing their broth with an equal quantity of sweet cream. To this, add butter-sautéed littlest cubes of celery,
sweet onion, and fennel, and as many herbs as you have. Mix in the
clams, spoon the mixture back into clean clamshells, cover generously
with fresh breadcrumbs, and bake until browned. I ate these every
Christmas when I was very young, cooked by a Sicilian neighbor

named Dolly. She followed them with artichoke pie and roasted lobster. I recommend the menu, in its entirety, for the bold and brave.

Here are three hors d'œuvres from the middle of last century or earlier that do not fit any mold. They are not as simple and affordable as plates of raw vegetables or pickles or roast oysters and clams. They are too costly, too filling, and too likely to be seen as putting on a show. They are exceptions—what might be called "birds without a branch"—included because they are too good to ignore.

My opposition to costly hors d'œuvres collapses before a 1950s-ish recipe that has the scrubbed innocence of a bowl of strong broth. It is made of steak, packaged white bread, and butter. None can be improved or fancified without somewhat trespassing on the virgin purity of the dish. It is to my knowledge made only in one household by an Aunt Julia, who I believe inherited the recipe from the Aunt Julia before her. I came by it via Aunt Julia's nephew, a dapper magazine writer whom I met at a cocktail party. I employed no intrigue or trickery, though I do wonder what Aunt Julia will think of her secrets being aired. The original recipe was for fifty. I have scaled it down, but otherwise left the recipe unchanged.

FILET MIGNON ON TOAST

1 whole beef tenderloin
kosher salt
pre-sliced, store-bought packaged white bread
½ cup (1 stick) salted butter

Here is a verbatim note: *"The bread is the butter-blood-steak delivery method, nothing more. We have used potato breads before, and as long as they're not too fancy, they work well. Pillowy, good juice absorption. The only times we've really failed this thing were when someone bought bread from an actual bakery."* Dry the tenderloin and salt very well. Let sit for 15 to 30 minutes at room temperature. Cook whole, on the grill or in a cast-iron pan, to medium-rare. Let rest for 10 minutes. Toast the bread until crisp.

Also verbatim: *"Melt butter in a saucepan. Remove from the heat. Add the blood that's accumulated on the plate where you've been keeping the steak. Slice the steak as thinly as possible. Cut the toast in halves or quarters. The pieces of toast should be only slightly larger than the pieces of steak, with the general rule being: one piece of steak for every piece of bread, until the tenderloin's tapered end, when doubling up is permitted. Dip each slice of steak in the butter-blood sauce, then onto a piece of toast. Once all the steak has been placed on the bread, drizzle the remaining butter-blood mixture over the toasts with a spoon. Serve on large platters. Eat on good china or standing up in the backyard."*

I believe that Aunt Julia's brood of fifty eats filet mignon on toast at Christmas. I have never served it at a large gathering for the same reason I have never cooked it as it is written. Faced with beef prices, I substitute New York strip—still pricey—for filet mignon, and produce it only for subdued groups of four. But I know in my heart that such subtle gatherings aren't proper, and vow to someday furnish the dish with the budget and the audience it deserves.

The next unperchable bird is braised lettuce on toast. Through the 1960s, lettuce on toast was as common as cake (or deviled eggs). But in the decade that followed, nutritionists and biochemists, licensed by the language of vitamins and minerals and conjugated linoleic acids and calories—in other words: science—determined that lettuce was *good for you*. Well-meaning mothers, trying to do right, inferred that lettuce should not be cooked, but eaten as medicine. Or that is my theory.

(In truth, this matter, like many in nutritional science, is gray: water-soluble vitamins may degrade in heat, fat-soluble ones may not; some vitaminic compounds are *more* digestible when heated. Less data exist for hot and cold lettuce than for carrots and broccoli, because lettuce is less often cooked . . . Regardless, any vegetable you eat is better for you than one you don't.

An almost magical effect is achieved when soft heat and butter are applied to fresh lettuce. The lettuce at first shudders, then surrenders, becoming a conduit for warm butter and a foil for crisp toast. It will turn a not-at-all-handsome shade of moss green, and it will taste of easy opulence. Note: The toast for this dish must be rather large, which should be kept in mind in planning the rest of the menu and for guests with delicate appetites.

BRAISED LETTUCE ON TOAST

1 large or 2 small heads romaine lettuce
18 anchovy fillets, roughly chopped
½ clove garlic, pounded to a paste with a little bit of salt
7 tablespoons unsalted butter, at room temperature
6 pieces rustic bread, about ½ inch thick, sliced in half crosswise
¼ cup chicken or vegetable stock
kosher or sea salt
zest of ½ lemon

Remove the outer leaves from the romaine, saving them for soup. Trim the bases, leaving the head(s) intact and leaves connected. Cut into 6 thin vertical wedges, connected at the base.

Make anchovy butter by pounding the anchovies to a paste with the garlic paste, then mashing in 4 tablespoons of the butter.

Toast the bread.

Warm a pan large enough to fit all the lettuce wedges. Add the remaining 3 tablespoons butter. Once it has melted, add the stock, and fit the romaine wedges closely into the pan in a single layer. Salt lightly. Cook over medium heat for about 2 minutes, then turn all the wedges to another side. Scatter with lemon zest. Continue to cook, turning once or twice more, until the liquid has been absorbed and the lettuce is very wilted and tender throughout. Turn off the heat.

On a cutting board, slice each wedge twice across to make for easier eating.

Spread the toast thickly with the anchovy butter and top with the lettuce. Serve hot.

Braised lettuce is good before simple second courses like poached or scrambled eggs, a salad or some favorite cheese, with good plain wine.

To serve this as a side dish instead of as an appetizer, eliminate the toast and serve the anchovy butter on top of, rather than under, the cooked lettuce. Then it will slump in muted poise beside fish meunière or roast chicken, or barbecued quails!

The final branchless bird is a canary. If you have bought its three ingredients, all inexorably finicky and fine, you are doomed, pointed down a chute of lost pleasures. You've put a bottle of Champagne on ice. There are boned quails with fat wild mushrooms to accompany them and a redolent cheese soufflé. There is a salad of herbs. Charlotte Russe is chilling. The efforts have been dizzying and renewing. You've gone all out, and think wistfully of those meals past with which you dealt in a thoroughly modern way, serving cheese and crackers, tacos, and frozen yogurt for dessert.

I offer this comfort: Serving a meal to which I condemned myself by beginning with these tiny sandwiches of foie gras, I have glimpsed on guests' faces hedonic delight previously unknown. I have watched them for a moment come to a sort of timeless understanding of their sensuous capacities. In other words, the strange human invention of hospitality has served a purpose for which the cost of my labors—not to mention foie gras—seems slight.

It cannot be as old as roast oysters, but this canary was probably eaten by ancient Egyptians—for whom goose liver and white bread were delicacies—and by whomever dined in the company of the Vicomte de Mauduit, who called small rounds of bread fried in tarragon butter, spread with foie gras, then shrimp, truffles, and watercress, *canapés à la Vicomte*. (The Vicomte also provided instruction for a more ordinary variation: *Spread some foie gras on slices of brown bread and butter and make into sandwiches*.) It certainly was eaten by diners here in centuries past, under the more cautious name of *foie gras canapés*. Anyway, its pleasures are so many, so ancient, so innocent, and so plain that . . . oh, but better just to try it for yourself. And toast your table with Seneca's old words: "When shall we live if not now?"

FOIE GRAS SANDWICHES

½ loaf *pain de mie* (fine-textured white bread)
1 can very best foie gras, or ½ lobe poached foie gras
best salted butter

Cut the crust from the pain de mie *and slice the bread thinly. Butter one side of each slice. Cut each into quarters. Layer foie gras thickly onto the dry sides of half the slices. Top with the remaining bread, buttered-side out. Brown the tiny sandwiches in a lightly buttered skillet on both sides, à la grilled cheese. Serve immediately.*

My hors d'œuvre prescriptions are, with some disagreeable insistence, for *one* hors d'œuvre. This is for my own aesthetic—and maybe ascetic—satisfaction. But you may be a person who finds yourself always on the bank of a truth: that one hors d'œuvre does not satisfy you because you like them more than you like anything else.

In that case, you must be unstinting. Serve crudités *and* gildas and roast oysters. And pickled shrimp and *aubergines en hors d'œuvre*. And what you find beneath stones left unturned by my inadequate survey of forgotten snacks: walnut-studded, cigarillo-sized salamis; cheeses wrapped in grape leaves and grilled; stuffed snails. The meal can end there, or with caviar-leek *pots de crème*, or the caviar alone, eaten on potato chips. I like hors d'œuvres in spoonfuls. But better advice than to follow me is to do what you want, choosing from what you have read and tasted and known, and make your meal wholly yours. That is most likely to result in your enjoying it, which is, after all, the point.

A FANCY
SPRING DINNER

Caviar-leek pots de crème

Wine: A rich, velvety, dry white
with plenty of acidity
Example: Chardonnay
Henri Germain Chassagne-Montrachet 2014

Green Goddess salad

Chicken à la Montmorency

Buttered green peas

Wine: A medium-bodied, floral,
cherry-toned red
Example: Nebbiolo
Burlotto Langhe Nebbiolo 2015

Shortbread

LA BONNE SOUPE

Soups

II

"Et hop! Par ici, la bonne soupe!"
("Step right up, and place a bet for the good
life!")

—Félicien Marceau

The spirit of the elemental liquids called soups is best understood by the long-gone housewives who knew it all: soups—whether Neolithic bouillon, medieval porridge, or more recent purées and bisques and consommés—have transcendental powers and should—I feel absurdly moved to write *must*—be eaten as often as possible. In comprehending French, *la bonne soupe* is a frank idiom for the good life—something like *la dolce vita*, but less voluptuous, more fatalistic, reflecting the culture that coined it.

To me, reflecting my own private culture, *la bonne soupe* will always be literal, referring to whatever hot redolent liquid in a ceramic pot my mother, who believes in transcendentalism only in soups, served most nights. It may have been thick or thin and it shaped my palate and probably—given how often we ate chicken broth and beef stew, barley soup and butternut potage, split pea and lentil, and the occasional worldly curried to-do—my mind.

Until the world became as small and fast as it now is, that was a universal truth: soup of some kind, often a slight variation on nutritious primordial broth, held at least subtle introductory sway, serving the dual or sometimes triple purpose of using up some bit left from an earlier meal, providing a transition for body and mind from the bites before a meal to the meat of the matter, and (sometimes) stretching a small amount of a delicacy far, as only the swimminess of soup will do.

This pattern held until the ceremonial visions of the Victorian age became industrial. The gilding on the Gilded Age dulled and chipped. Dining became less formal. The category of soups sprang leaks.

Today, soup is practical or it is extinct: minestrone of a thousand varieties is easy enough to come by. So are kale and potato, chorizo and clam, black bean, pork belly ramen, chicken and rice, and Texas chili.

Those are all good and deserve the nominally positive designation of "hearty." The *bonne* soups that have disappeared from menus are mostly simple and understated combinations of light leafy things, broths and muted bisques, consommés, and "creams"—soups invented in a distant frame within which anything might become a soup, because a soup there would be.

Of these, the most lovely and ghostly is herb soup, a version of which seeded menus through the 1950s—in part because any vegetable with a leafy aspect or plant with a human use might be called "herb," the category being not botanical but teleological.

Here is an old recipe for this adaptable soup, provided half for literary value, from the 1615 *The English Husewife*.

POTTAGE: (Vegetable ingredients): Violet leaves (petals), Succory, Strawberry leaves, Spinage, Langdebeef (a variety of bugloss), Marygold flowers, Scallions, and a little Parsley, (with oatmeal added to the kettle.)

The large, heavy 1832 *Cook's Own Book* supplies an herb soup recipe calling for cabbages, carrots, chervil, purslane, parsley, sorrel, cucumbers, and a crust of bread stewed in hot water and butter, enriched with egg yolks and cream. A tenuously alluring *Stock for Herb* from the 1753 *The Lady's Companion* combines regular kitchen garden vegetables with chervil and "sweet herbs" and "strain[s] out the Liquor through a Seive . . ."

For actually cooking—and moreover eating—I like the following herb soup, which is simple but unusual. Among the herb soup recipes in my library, it deserves the unique distinction of producing a recognizable soup of herbs.

HERB SOUP

3 tablespoons olive oil, plus more for drizzling, if desired
2 stalks celery, thinly sliced
1 leek, white and light green parts, thinly sliced and well
    washed
1½ teaspoons kosher salt, plus to taste
3 cloves spring garlic, or 1 clove winter garlic
½ to 1 teaspoon garam masala
¼ teaspoon cayenne pepper
4 cups water
8 cups mixed fresh soft herbs (cilantro, basil, Thai basil, sorrel,
    chervil), stemmed and roughly chopped
2 tablespoons heavy cream
optional: fresh lemon juice

Heat a soup pot, add the olive oil, and cook the celery and leek until wilted, adding salt at the start. Add the garlic, garam masala, and cayenne, and stir through. (If you like the queasily rich taste of garam masala, add a full teaspoon. I waver.) Cook the vegetables until completely tender, adding a little water if they start to brown.

Add the water to the pot. Taste the broth. It should be quite heavily seasoned. Adjust as needed. Add the herbs and immediately turn off the heat. Mix the herbs through. Add the cream. Blend to the smoothness you like—I like it opulently smooth, which sometimes demands a final straining through a sieve. Serve hot or cold, drizzled with lemon juice or good olive oil, if desired.

From one's own garden the combination would tip toward cilantro or sorrel, which both grow like weeds. It could be called in that instance a weed soup, truthfully, if not invitingly. It can be made as plush as a featherbed by adding more cream, up to ½ cup, or as plain as the *Lady's Companion's* by omitting cream entirely, according to the cook's mood.

Likely to slip down certain throats even more smoothly is this "Soup Herb Spirit" from the 1846 *The American Kitchen Directory and Housewife* by Ann House:

Those who like a variety of herbs in soup, will find it very convenient to have the following mixture. Take when in their prime, thyme, sweet marjoram, sweet basil, and summer savory. When thoroughly dried, pound and sift them. Steep them in brandy for a fortnight, the spirit will then be fit for use.

For use in what? The apothecary doesn't say. It sounds like an unusually stimulating analeptic, and I plan to brew a flask in spring. Or, if I am feeling indolent or Zen, perhaps I will place my soup bowl carefully and await this soup, from Basho: *Under the cherry-/blossom soup,/blossom salad*—which sounds like a meal for the satyrs, and for me.

Today's average kitchen hutch is not stocked with many small soup plates that are the right size for serving the smooth first-course soups of yesteryear.

I have two ways to solve the problem. First is to serve hot soup in great-grandmother's china teacups or another unconventional vessel smaller than a soup bowl, and cold soup in highball glasses, to be sipped like some exotic juice. There is innate charm to eating soup out of a piece of dinnerware meant for something else. A second strategy is to buy soup plates, but the less acquisitive resolution is an honorable one, and puts teacups and glass tumblers to good use.

One sadly extinct soup that diminishes in charm as it increases in quantity is potent, soothing watercress soup. For the British and French—and us, who borrowed so much culinary convention from them—this fairy-green cream was for two hundred years probably the most common soup after nursery porridge. Watercress could be picked beside streams, and its light piquancy was still indestructive to the overall blandness much in favor.

One of the many drawbacks to the desertion of watercress soup is the disappearance of the culinary intelligence attached to it. A handful of eye-stinging watercress, whether from a stream bank or a bin at your local Korean grocery, makes of a dispassionate soup of onion, potato, and water something delicious. This improvement is inexpensive and looks fetching in teacups.

WATERCRESS SOUP

1 medium white or yellow onion, diced
3 tablespoons unsalted butter
1 teaspoon sea salt, plus to taste
5 cups water
½ pound potatoes, diced
2 bunches watercress, thoroughly cleaned and roughly chopped
1 teaspoon fresh lemon juice
¼ cup heavy cream

Cook the onion in the butter until softened, adding the salt at the start. Add some of the water if it threatens to brown. When the onion is tender, add the potatoes and remaining water. Cook for about 20 minutes, until the potatoes are tender and break easily with a spoon. Add the watercress and cook for 2 to 3 minutes. Add the lemon juice. Add the cream. Cool to room temperature. Blend in batches until very smooth and, if you like, pass through a very fine sieve—which is both messy and perhaps essential for total smoothness (though total smoothness, of course, is not essential). Reheat without boiling or chill further and serve cold.

Watercress soup is best with leftover cooked lima beans or poached shrimp or a handful of crisp croutons, left from another meal, plopped in a mound in the soup saucer's middle. Those, or other little additions, have the effect of making the soup seem both smoother and more vegetal.

There are almost endless variants on this basic method, which, taken together, form the foggy category of *velouté* or *crème* or "cream of _____." If potatoes are the soup's focus, you have a *velouté de pomme de terre*, or cream of potato. For a cream of green pea, add a quarter as many potatoes and replace the missing potatoes with peas once the potatoes are tender. Stop cooking when the peas begin to pucker, add a small handful of mint or chervil or parsley, and proceed as on page 49. The basic method for cream of corn is identical, using corn. Thinking this way, you might make cream of broccoli, or cream of cauliflower, or cream of asparagus or turnip, or, or, or.

A literal mind asks why these ancestral soups are "creams" of anything. Their main ingredients release only their own vegetal juices—not cream—when pressed. The lexical confusion owes to soup names once coming from French, in which creamy soups made somewhat according to this pattern are called either *velouté* or *crème*. (Classical books are endlessly dogmatic. *Crème* is finished with cream, and *velouté* is finished with a *liaison* of cream and egg yolks.) They are named for their techniques, not exertions of or upon their ingredients.

If one's cream of potato soup began with a stately leek, is well adorned with cream, chilled, and perhaps accessorized with a spattering of chives, it is vichyssoise, once taken for health at Vichy, then for status at the Plaza.

I served my own variant on vichyssoise every other night for a month when I ran a restaurant in Athens, Georgia. It conferred no status on anyone, for it was born of a sensible and firmly practical system: I served mashed leeks and potatoes Monday, Wednesday, and Friday nights. Tuesday, Thursday, and Saturday mornings, I put what was left through a fine food mill, added cream to the resulting purée, diligently chilled it, and garnished it abundantly. I found this such an economical and fine arrangement that my most honest recipe for vichyssoise is: "Pass leftover mashed potatoes through a fine mill and add cream." For more rigorous instruction, there exist numerous excellent examples in cookbooks old and new.

The best-known variant on this theme is cream of tomato. The old-fashioned version's combination of canned tomato, onion, flour, and milk—dating to the early years of last century—has survived charitably in collective memory, and in some kitchens. The speed and economy with which it can be produced ensure that mothers still make it thus for young children, stamping onto growing minds that formula for cream of tomato soup as an eternal symbol of the days when they were cooked *for*, in other words, when they were Young.

I do not have that symbol imprinted on my palate and mind. My mother never made cream of tomato soup. I take secondhand pleasure, though, in reading of variations in old housewifery and Ladies' Aid Society books. As long as they call for fresh cream—not condensed milk—and tomatoes—not tomato sauce—the old recipes are basically fine and reliably produce what most people miss—other than youth, for which the manuals offer no suggestions.

For a very different cream of tomato soup, I like the following. I first tasted it when I was between old and young, one hot early morning in Cordoba, Spain . . . and felt comprehending and comforted in a hundred ways outside and in. It is even more economical than the American one, relying on stale bread instead of cream, and just as efficient to make. It is what all children I cook for will think of when in later life they hear the sentimental summons of "cream of tomato . . ."

COLD CREAM OF TOMATO SOUP (SALMOREJO)

about 2 pounds good, ripe tomatoes
2 cloves garlic, roughly chopped
¼ cup good sherry or red wine vinegar
½ pound crustless stale peasant bread, in slices or pieces

kosher salt
1 to 2 cups very good olive oil
optional: chopped hard-cooked eggs, shreds of Spanish ham,
    croutons for garnish

Cut out the hard portion near the stem of each tomato, saving any juice. In a blender, working in batches, blend the garlic, sherry, some stale bread, and a small pinch of salt. Add some tomatoes and blend further. Then add more bread and tomatoes and any saved juice. In a slow, steady stream, add 1 cup of the olive oil, dividing it in half if you are doing two batches due to blender size. Decide whether to add more olive oil by tasting. It should be quite thick and rich, but not sticky, and to your liking. Add more olive oil, slowly, stopping when your instincts say to. When all the ingredients are blended, taste for salt and vinegar and adjust. Serve this chilled, topped with any or all of the optional garnishes, or just an additional drizzle of olive oil.

In his fine 1960 *The Queen Cookery Book*, Ambrose Heath wrote of a French tomato soup "or shall we call them *'pommes d'amour*,' since there is an indigenous connection between this soup and the marriage bed." Is there? *Salmorejo* is energizing, but I can't say to what end.

I have, in winter, sacrilegiously served it hot, after finding a batch in the corner of my freezer. Topped with crisp croutons and fried ham, it was savorous, if not aphrodisiacal.

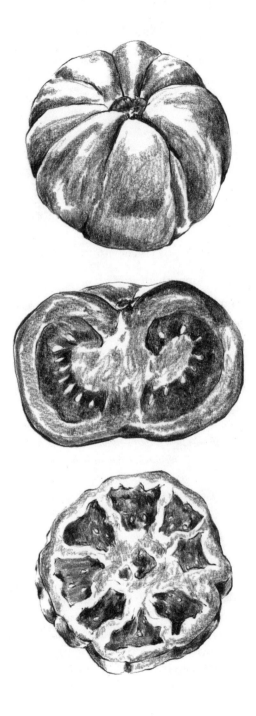

Probably the lightest of this category is cream of lettuce soup—which once went by titles as regal as a tiara: *lettuce à la crème, lettuce à la reine*, cream of lettuce Bostonienne, velouté of lettuce Sevigné. It is, nonetheless, a simple soup for simple tastes.

CREAM OF LETTUCE SOUP

4 tablespoons (½ stick) salted butter
1 small onion or white part of 1 leek, chopped or sliced
kosher salt
handful of fresh parsley, chervil, or cilantro, or 8 to 10 fresh
    tarragon leaves
3 to 4 cups water
2 or 3 heads Boston, romaine, or other green leaf lettuce (about
    ¾ pound), chopped
optional: 2 tablespoons heavy cream
optional: little croutons, for garnish

Melt half the butter and sauté the onion, adding salt at the start, over medium-low heat until completely tender, adding a little water if it threatens to brown. Add the herbs and mix through. Add the water, bring to a boil, then add the lettuce and lower the heat to a simmer. Cook for 2 minutes. Purée in batches in a blender until completely smooth (be careful—it will be hot). Return to the pot over low heat and add the remaining 2 tablespoons butter and the cream, if using. Season with salt. Serve hot or cold, garnished, if you like, with little croutons.

The whole operation is quick, and the result even better the next day. Improvisation is welcome: a handful of English peas or asparagus or asparagus *bottoms* give lettuce soup more substance. Add and subtract as needed, as long as things stay simple.

A restrained hand is also the key to the rather pontifically named *potage Esau.* This soup of butter, herbs, water, and lentils is as old as the Bible, from which it gets its name. It has been eaten for all history since, but in fat days between then and now, some indiscretion plagued the old decent soup. Craig Claiborne and Pierre Franey published a recipe in the *New York Times* in 1981, calling for salt pork fat, butter, heavy cream, and eleven cups of beef broth(!). The resulting porridge is fun to read about but impossible to eat. Here is a more possible one that is still good for meals, as Irish writer Maura Laverty says, "when the main course is not too sure of itself."

POTAGE ESAU

2 tablespoons olive oil
1 small onion, diced
1 small carrot, diced
2 tablespoons finely chopped fresh rosemary or sage or
    marjoram
2 cloves garlic, minced
2 teaspoons kosher salt, or to taste
1 pound brown lentils
bouquet garni of parsley stems, thyme, and a bay leaf
10 cups water
5 tablespoons unsalted butter
4 cups finely sliced fresh sorrel
½ cup finely chopped fresh parsley
dry sherry or red wine vinegar, for serving
freshly ground black pepper

In a large pot, heat the olive oil and sauté the onion, carrot, rosemary, and garlic with a sprinkle of salt until mostly tender, about 5 minutes. Add the lentils, bouquet garni, remaining salt, and water. Bring to a boil, then lower to a simmer, skimming off any scum that rises to the top. Cook at a very low simmer for about 1 hour, or until the lentils are completely tender and taste delicious. Remove the bouquet garni. In batches, purée about three-quarters of the soup in a blender until quite smooth (be careful—it will be hot).

In the now empty pot, melt 3 tablespoons of the butter. Add the sorrel and parsley. Cook for 1 to 3 minutes, until the sorrel has wilted and lost its color. Add the puréed soup, the unpuréed lentils, and remaining 2 tablespoons butter to the pot, gently stirring in the remaining butter as it heats.

Serve very hot, with sherry sprinkled onto each bowl and freshly ground
black pepper on top.

A cream soup made according to a different technique is clam
chowder. Clam chowder as we know it today may have been brought
here by settlers of Rhode Island or Maine or New York, or it may
have been made earlier and more plainly by the Narragansett natives.
When clams were not thought inconvenient for their shells—or unat-
tractive for their ubiquity—clam chowder had many variants and
many homes.

I have never met the mythical people who argue, incensed by
criminal alternatives, that chowder must be thickened with cracker
crumbs. Or with flour. Or contain only clams, sweet butter, and
milk. Or be made with tomato. (In the appraisal of an older friend,
they may all be dead or reduced to an enclave on Martha's Vineyard.
A friend of *his*, who grew up on the Vineyard, recently put oyster
crackers in a fish chowder the two were eating "as if there were no
other way to eat it," and said people on the Vineyard still care.) The
two people I have seen in regular dialogue on the merits of different
approaches to chowder—my grandparents—inhabited opposite ends
of the spectrum—she liking it creamy and white, he with tomato
under the stiff name Manhattan—and were in love.

In any case, the soup has had centuries if not millennia in which
to be made all ways—even perhaps, in some ecstatic household, all
at once!

Here is a recipe for the clam chowder called "New England." At
least that's what it was called at the Maine restaurants we went to when
I was a child, with names like The Candlestick and The Blue Moose.

CLAM CHOWDER

5 pounds littleneck or cherrystone clams
½ cup good white wine
1 cup water
1 clove garlic
1 dried chile

bottled clam juice (buy 2 bottles, though you may only use 1)
2 slices bacon, chopped
2 tablespoons unsalted butter
½ cup chopped celery
½ cup chopped onion
kosher salt
½ pound yellow potatoes, peeled or unpeeled, chopped
bouquet garni of parsley stems, sprigs of fresh thyme, a little
      rosemary, a bay leaf
optional: 2 cups fresh or frozen corn kernels
1 cup heavy cream
2 tablespoons mixed chopped fresh chives and parsley
optional: freshly ground black pepper

In a big heavy pot, combine the clams, wine, water, garlic, and chile and bring to a boil. Remove the clams as they open, one by one, to a waiting plate or bowl. Discard any that do not open after 7 minutes. Remove the clam meat from the shells, saving any accumulated broth. Strain all the clam broth into a measuring cup through a fine-mesh strainer twice, or through cheesecloth once. Add enough bottled clam juice to make 4 cups. Chop the clams.

In the same pot, cook the bacon in the butter until mostly rendered. Remove some fat from the pot if desired. Add the celery and onion, salting at the start. Cook until the vegetables can be broken with a spoon. Add the clam broth, potatoes, and bouquet garni. Bring to a boil, then lower the heat to a simmer. Skim off any scum that rises to the top. Cook until the potatoes are completely tender, about 20 minutes. Add the corn, if using, and simmer for 1 minute. Add the chopped clams and cream. Taste for salt. Add the herbs and serve hot, seasoned with freshly ground black pepper, if desired.

It should be noted that of all of yesterday's soups, clam chowder probably has the most in common with today's. It has minestrone's malleability—if you have fish instead of clams, a summer or winter squash instead of potatoes, and scallions instead of onions, they can be substituted unthinkingly and make a good soup and, moreover, depending on your definition, a good *chowder*. To become a meal, any variation needs only crackers or good bread, some sort of salad, and maybe an appealingly kitschy "New England" dessert like baked apples (cores scooped out and replaced with oats, brown sugar, and butter, and baked) or Indian pudding . . .

What can be said of oyster stew, other than that it has been unfairly wiped from cookbook pages?

It is perhaps worth adding some detail. For most of this land's history, and certainly in 1931, when Irma S. Rombauer first gave broad readership *The Joy of Cooking*, oyster stew was as brawny a category of soup as "Cream of" or "Canned." The table of contents of her second edition divides soups into Cream Soups, Oyster Stews, Canned Soup Recipes, and so on. But as the oyster was sent rumbling from New York and Wilmington to Des Moines, the soups that relied on it diminished nearly as quickly as oyster stocks did. (Now the oyster population is to my—and, one imagines, its—happiness growing and improving. Oysters are being seeded heartily in many of the very tidal inlets where they once flourished by nature.)

Oyster stew still *exists*, but other than sitting at the Grand Central Oyster Bar, pushing the high price from one's mind, and giving in to the old simplicity of a man with dexterous hands shucking oysters and tipping them into a copper urn with melted butter, a long pour of cream, a shake of paprika, and a dash of sherry, the way to get it is to make it oneself. This is worth doing, every now and again, especially when there are only two or three of you. It is very fast for so few eaters, and the sweet salinity of the oyster and the bland richness of the cream are a perennially good match.

OYSTER STEW

4 to 6 oysters per person
1½ tablespoons butter per person
½ shallot, minced, per person
½ to ⅔ cup whole milk per person
½ cup heavy cream per person
1 bay leaf

¼ teaspoon kosher salt, plus more to taste, per person
a small handful of finely chopped parsley
freshly ground black pepper
soda crackers or buttered toast, for serving

Shuck the oysters directly into a fine sieve over a bowl. In a small pot, heat 1 tablespoon of the butter, and cook the shallot with the salt until completely tender, 3 to 5 minutes. Add the milk, cream, bay leaf, and oyster liquid. Bring to just below a simmer for 1 minute, taste, and adjust the salt. Add the oysters and remaining butter and cook for 1 to 2 minutes, until they just plump. Immediately pour the stew into small waiting bowls, removing the bay leaf and adding parsley and a grind of black pepper and accompanying with crackers or toast.

This encouraging brew is especially appropriate to several circumstances: First is when you are very tired. Someone among you must not be tired and moreover willing to shuck oysters. But if there is such a hardy being, beseech him or her, for your weary soul needs succor and this stew provides it. Oyster stew is also a hangover cure on par with the Mexican *menudo* or Provençal *aigo bouido* or Parisian onion soup. It heals fatigue and "breeds optimism." So, second is the morning. Then, you need an even hardier companion—willing to face a fish smell, brittle shells, and a sharp knife with a headache. If you're lucky enough to have such a friend, keep him or her near; they are few. Third is midafternoon in winter, when you are tormented with the desperate feeling that can come with cold-weather hunger.

For the third case, here are tips from the third of Mrs. Rombauer's oyster stew recipes, which she calls "the little bear, the big bear, and the great big bear." Her first is like mine. Her second somewhat like it. For the great big bear she melts butter alone in a pot and adds flour, stirring until golden, then adds oyster liquor. This makes a stew to stick to your bones and quell desperation. For serving instructions I offer these, from Gary Snyder's "How to Make Stew in the Pinacate Desert": "Dish it up and eat it with a spoon, sitting on a poncho in the dark."

In his *Dictionary of Cuisine*, Alexandre Dumas defined *bisque* as "the most royal of dishes . . . a food for princes and financiers." Of the occupations humans have devised, neither aristocracy nor banking seems most regal. Both are often, in fact, among the most depraved . . .

But I like bisque. This bisque is for fishermen and boatbuilders, for mothers and fathers, toll collectors, bricklayers, cooks, floor cleaners, window washers, bakers, bookbinders, gas pump attendants, metal-workers, and teachers, a most noble if not royal collection of humanity indeed.

SHRIMP BISQUE

1 pound shrimp, peeled and deveined, shells reserved
bouquet garni of a bay leaf, a few thyme stems, and a few
    parsley stems
8 cups water
kosher salt
4 tablespoons olive oil
3 tablespoons sherry or dry white wine
1 small shallot, diced
½ clove garlic, minced
¼ cup Arborio, Carnaroli, or Vialone Nano rice
¼ cup heavy cream
handful of chopped fresh parsley and/or cilantro
optional: drizzle of amontillado sherry
freshly ground black pepper
optional: tiny crisp croutons

Put the shrimp shells, bouquet garni, and water in a medium pot. Bring to a boil, lower the heat to maintain a low simmer, and cook for 25 to 30 minutes, until the stock tastes delicately of shrimp. (Put a few grains of salt into the spoon when you taste. This will help your judgment.) Strain the stock and discard the shells. Meanwhile, heat a pan large enough to hold all the shrimp. Add 2 tablespoons of the olive oil, then the shrimp, and salt them lightly. Cook until pink on the bottom—about 1 minute—then turn. Cook for about 20 seconds, then add the sherry.

Cook until the alcohol has burned off and the shrimp are just cooked, 30 seconds to 1 minute. Cool and chop. In a medium pot, cook the shallot in the remaining 2 tablespoons olive oil, salting lightly. When mostly tender, add the garlic, stir through, cook a few seconds to soften, then add the shrimp stock and rice. Cook at a boil until the rice is completely swollen and tender, about 20 minutes. Add three-quarters of the shrimp and the cream and blend with a handheld blender or a standing one until completely smooth, adding sprinkles of water if it is too thick. Taste and adjust the salt. To serve, return to the barest simmer, add a drizzle of amontillado sherry, if desired, and adjust the thickness and salt to your liking. Serve very hot, topped with shrimp, the herbs, black pepper, and any other garnishes.

People who write about soup are worth listening to, especially when they enter a missionary mood. Ambrose Heath, author of a hundred or so cookbooks, including *Good Soups* and *Soups and Soup Garnishes*, is a particular tonic to the jaded recipe reader, with his small pronouncements of support for soups he thinks good, like onion ("the soup of soups"!) and mussel, whose central bivalves he calls, somewhat evangelistically, "particularly good soup makers."

There is one mussel soup, from 1925, unusual for containing, by the time it reaches the soup plate, no mussels. According to legend, *potage Billy By*, as it came to be called, was first served by Louis Barthe at Ciro's in Deauville to friends of a wealthy American named William Brand who wanted to protect them from the rough French habit of eating mussels from the shell with one's hands. Barthe served the Americans bowls of mussel broth enriched with herbs, aromatics, and cream, with the mussels reserved for another use, and for the rest of their visit the Americans stopped by, asking for *potage William Brand*, which ended up on the menu as the more discreet *potage Billy By*. The shrewd Barthe brought the soup to Maxim's, where it became locally famous. The *New York Times*' Craig Claiborne published a recipe for it by Pierre Franey, in 1961, adding his own evangelical exordium: "This may well be the most elegant and delicious soup ever created." I don't know. But it is good.

POTAGE BILLY BY

1 stalk celery, chopped (nearly ½ cup)
½ cup chopped fennel
1 cup chopped sweet onion
3 tablespoons olive oil
1 bay leaf
bouquet garni of fresh thyme, parsley stems, 2 strips orange peel
     (peeled with a vegetable peeler), and basil if it is summer
large pinch of saffron
2 dried chiles
3 pounds good fresh mussels
1 cup white wine
2 cups fish stock, clam juice, or water
¼ to 1 cup heavy cream
1 lemon

Sweat the celery, fennel, and onion in the olive oil in a wide heavy pot. Add the bay leaf, bouquet garni, saffron, chiles, mussels, and wine to the pot, turn the heat to high, cover, and cook until the mussels open, 2 to 7 minutes, removing them as they do. Discard any that do not open after 7 minutes.

    Remove the mussels from their shells, returning all the broth they've retained to the pot, and reserving them for another use. Add the fish stock to the broth and cook until the broth has reduced to about 4 cups. Strain through two layers of fine cheesecloth into a bowl and return to the pot. Add the cream, stopping when the soup tastes good to you. Serve immediately, with a few drops of lemon juice per bowl. Or, to serve cold, chill for at least 2 hours.

In addition to being elegant—and delicious—*potage Billy By* is an ingenious way to get one batch of mussels to produce two dishes. For a meal of subtle continuity, serve the mussels themselves next, lightly marinated in lemon and herbs (see the recipe for pickled shrimp, page 21). Another way to stay on the same wave is to substitute cooked mussels for scallops for a baffling but esculent *coquilles St-Jacques* (page 209).

As far as I know, there is not an oysterless oyster soup on the books. But I have found one such specimen with clams, in the Honorable Mrs. Lionel Guest's 1918 *Soup, Oysters & Surprises*. I know only a single phrase that accurately describes its taste—from Elizabeth Bishop's North Haven journals: "It is light but ponderous." Here it is as Mrs. Guest wrote it:

Clam Bouillon for 8 People

Take three cupsful of clams, chop them, and put them in a saucepan with their liquor. Scald them, skim the top, and add three cupsful of boiling water, a tablespoon of chopped celery, an equal amount of chopped parsley, a mace, salt, pepper, and paprika. Boil, skim, and strain. Serve in cups with whipped cream on the top.

Mrs. Guest's recipe is good, and stands on its own feet as long as one knows a few things: about eight pounds of clams in their shells produce three cups of clam meat. The eight pounds should be steamed open in a few cups of water and a splash of wine and the meat removed from the shells, then ¾ to 1 cup water added at the end. A light grating of a nutmeg, if you like it, is simpler than hunting down whole mace. There is no need to "scald" anything, but only skim any scum that rises. And I, personally, leave out the paprika, because I love the monkish simplicity of just clam and whipped cream, a strange wonderful superfluity . . .

Another casual, warming bouillon soup is egg drop.

Egg drop soup became popular when Americans became fascinated by the habits of Chinese rail workers who arrived in the nineteenth century. The fascination grew into an affected contagion for Eastern culinary ways—steaming vegetables, clear sauces, stir-frying—which bore a whole series of cross-cultural mutts of Chinese technique and provincial American tastes and ingredients—like chop suey, crab rangoon, and wonton strips.

Egg drop soup is in the middle—neither precisely authentic to a single region of China nor any more unlikely to be made by a Chinese housewife than its Italian counterpart, *stracciatella*, or the French one, *le tourin*, would be in its homeland. It is as economical, agreeable, and sustaining as all the crude calming soups of its ilk. Indeed, it is a small irony of egg drop soup that it was once admired for its exoticism. It is, for the most part, a soup of pantry staples. If there is no cilantro or ginger, they may be omitted (though I have taken to keeping a knot of ginger in the house and find it gets used). If there is neither Shaoxing wine nor sherry, white vinegar can stand in. Otherwise, it is a soup of stock—which may be kept frozen—garlic, cornstarch, and eggs.

EGG DROP SOUP

4 cups chicken stock
½ cup water
1 clove garlic, sliced
12(ish) sprigs cilantro
1 (3-inch) piece fresh ginger, sliced
20(ish) peppercorns
kosher salt
1 tablespoon plus 1 teaspoon cornstarch
1 tablespoon Shaoxing wine or dry sherry
2 eggs
4 scallions, white and light green parts, sliced thinly on an angle
freshly ground white or black pepper

Put the chicken stock, water, garlic, cilantro, ginger, and peppercorns in a pot. Bring to a boil, then lower to a simmer. Cook for 20 minutes. Strain into a clean pot, taste, and adjust the salt. Bring back to a simmer. In a bowl, whisk together 1 tablespoon of the cornstarch with the wine. Whisk the eggs with the remaining 1 teaspoon cornstarch. Whisk the wine-cornstarch mixture into the soup. With the soup at a low simmer, stir with a wooden spoon to make a slight current. Slowly add the egg-cornstarch mixture, pouring it through the tines of a fork and letting it form ribbons. Allow to set for 10 seconds, then stir gently to break the ribbons as you like.

Top thickly with the scallions, season with pepper, and serve.

In my house, egg drop soup is dinner, especially if there are leftover cooked greens that can be dipped with tolerable impoliteness (and no authenticity) directly into each soup bowl. Or you might add some shredded chicken, or thinly sliced pork, cooked directly in the soup for a few minutes at the end. If this soup is to be a first course, some Eastward-looking second should follow it: poached chicken with a cilantro-ginger-scallion dipping sauce, or pork chops dusted with that faux Chinese trick: five-spice powder. If it is autumn, there should be persimmons for dessert.

"Soups are given many enticing names," wrote Irma Rombauer. None is so enticing to my ear as the slightly pneumatic *con-som-mé*. (It sounds, as soufflé does, like a fainting beauty. Soufflé's onomatopoetic quality, though, has some grounding. Without the accent, the word means "a low whistling sound." "Consomme" resists such etymologic sympathies, referring only to strong broth.) It is an enticing word and a captivating substance—the most basic of enhanced liquids, at once notable for its antiquity and artful simplicity.

It is also confusing: How is consommé different from stock and bouillon? And, today's worldly cook wonders, from Japanese dashi or Chinese *qing tang* or the rather less euphonious "bone broth," which has developed a cultish popularity of late? And what is the difference between *consommé madrilène*, *consommé Brillat-Savarin*, *consommé Colbert, Léopold, Monte-Carlo, Princess Alice,* and *Flor-ette* . . . ?!

I hope it is comforting to hear that the last few are all the same thing, served differently, some topped with little strips of crêpe, some with tiny vegetables, some with artichoke hearts and lettuce, some with rice and cream and Parmesan cheese.

I do not know, myself, what makes infusions of seaweed and dried fish and strong Chinese broth *them.* From my own culinary educa-tion, a broth that is not clear is just a broth—*bouillon* in French. It is an ingredient to be cooked with. Once the labor to clarify it has been dedicated, and a cook rewarded with a clarified broth, he or she may apply the term *consommé* and serve his or her effort, garnished or not, to be sipped.

That is official policy. I break with tradition. I believe in serving a broth that *tastes* good, whether or not it is "clear," rather than keeping good broth aside for solo consumption because it is not officially "con-sommé." My impertinent advice is, should you find yourself with a good-tasting stock that isn't translucent, and you are not in the mood to make it that way, to hold your head high and serve it as *consommé du maison.*

Here is traditional consommé instruction from Mme. Georgette Farkas, who presides over Rôtisserie Georgette, a high-ceilinged din-ing room on the Upper East Side of Manhattan. Mme. Georgette loves consommé with the genteel passion of the Raphaelite aristocrats she resembles. Hers is amber, translucent, rich as steak, and light as silk. The goal is "delicacy yet depth of flavor, a crystal clear broth that pleasantly coats the inside of the mouth."

I advise further cutting an important corner: wait to do this until you have a flavorful stock on hand—one made of duck or goose from Christmas dinner, or strong-boned laying hens, bought from the farmer. Then begin halfway, with the remaining distance not a great one at all. The important thing, as the essayist Aldo Buzzi once wrote, "is that the stock should be extra special, as it always is in poor countries: like Mexico and the Abruzzi . . ."

GEORGETTE'S CONSOMMÉ
(OR SOMETHING LIKE IT)

4 chicken carcasses or 3 pounds meaty chicken bones or backs
1 leek top
1 clove garlic
1 bay leaf
10(ish) parsley stems
12 cups chicken stock, duck stock, or mixed-species stock
a few black peppercorns, lightly crushed
1 teaspoon coarse sea salt
¼ pound ground white meat turkey
½ leek, chopped and well washed
¼ stalk celery, chopped
4 button mushrooms, cleaned
3 egg whites and eggshells
kosher salt
amontillado sherry

*Heat the oven to 325 degrees. Roast the chicken bones on baking sheets
until golden brown. Put the bones, leek top, garlic, bay leaf, and parsley
stems in a stockpot and cover with the stock, adding water as needed to
cover everything. Bring to a simmer, then reduce the heat and cook for
2 to 4 hours, until the roasted bones have lost their color. Strain through
a fine-mesh sieve into a bowl. Refrigerate. Once completely cool, skim
the fat from the top.*

*Meanwhile, to make the raft, combine the peppercorns, coarse sea salt,
turkey, leek, celery, mushrooms, and egg whites and shells in a food processor and process for 1 minute, stopping to scrape down if needed.*

*Combine the stock and raft in a pot that is taller than it is wide.
Bring to a slow boil over medium heat, stirring, until the raft becomes
a soft crust, 7 to 10 minutes. Once it has, make a hole in the center and
baste the raft occasionally, ladling liquid through the hole onto the raft.
Simmer over low heat without stirring until the liquid through the hole
appears completely clarified, 20 to 30 minutes. Set a sieve lined with
4 to 5 layers of cheesecloth over a bowl. Ladle the consommé through*

the hole in the raft into the sieve. Once it becomes impossible to retrieve
more, lift off the raft with a slotted spoon and carefully strain the rest
through even finer cheesecloth, into a separate bowl, if you are con-
cerned with absolute translucence. Season with salt and sherry.

"As for the garnish," Mme. Georgette says, "my seventh edition
Aide-Mémoire du Sommelier, closely guarded since Lausanne Hotel
School days, lists sixty-four classic consommé garnishes. In fall, here,
we add a wild mushroom ravioli and a few sprigs of tarragon. In win-
ter, it's foie gras ravioli. In spring, a brunoise of seasonal vegetables.
And no matter the garnish, I always add sherry."

Her garnishes of ravioli are whimsical and moreover delicious, but
just as lovely is a scattering of good herbs, or a spoonful of diced celery and fennel, boiled in salty water, added to each cup of consommé.
This keeps effort minimal and is as pretty as an English garden in
June.

And what of the other old soups, long ago forgotten? There are
thousands, tens of thousands, a number known only to the archivists.
What of the true exotics? Like the snail broth from *The Williamsburg
Art of Cookery* (originally from Martha Bradley's *The British Housewife*): "Pick twenty Garden Snails out of their shells and pound them
in a marble Mortar; take the hinder Legs of thirty Frogs, pound them
with the Snails . . ." What of those even more lost, like "Old-Fashioned
Scrap Soup," *soup maigre,* "Common Soup," and "Nutritious Soup for
the Laborious Poor"? All these have invisibly survived, because they
are soups of necessity, and continue to be made wherever humans
really need to eat.

There remains as ever a grain of truth in the valuation of soup
by the twelfth-century Italian Giovanni of Milan, who wrote, "Soup
makes teeth white and our eyes clear, fills the stomach and helps
digestion." And if it filled the mind with wisdom and heart with
compassion, we would have no need for civilization's more complex
contrivances.

A SUMMER LUNCH

Cucumbers with ravigote sauce

Cold cream of tomato soup

Mon Pierre's steak haché

Fried potatoes

Wine: An earthy, structured
yet vibrantly racy rosé
Example: Bandol
Château Pradeaux Bandol Rosé 2016

Fruit

A GROWING LOVE

Salads

III

My vegetable love should grow / Vaster than
empires and more slow.
> —Andrew Marvell, "To His Coy Mistress"

It has always seemed to me that human opinion makes no impression at all on plants' own intrinsic preferences. Vegetables know deep within their cells what they like. Combinations of them that taste good do because their components grow well together and get along.

One fine formula that has probably been with us since biblical times is well preserved in Chicago's Edgewater Beach Hotel's 1934 *Salad Book*.

Poor Man's Salad: Dandelions,
Cress, Chives, Garlic:

Mix equal quantities of very young dandelions and watercress. Rub a bowl with a clove of garlic or sprinkle a few chopped chives over herbs. Serve with French dressing.

It bears mentioning to today's cooks—who do not perhaps know it innately—that a "French dressing" is a vinaigrette, made inviolably with one part red or white wine vinegar to three parts oil. A thorough guide should also remind a contemporary salad maker to lightly salt the small wild leaves and the basic dressing, too, and to occasionally add a scrape of smooth Dijon mustard, mixed briskly into the vinegar before the olive oil.

The "Poor Man's Salad" recipe is accompanied in the *Salad Book* by this note: "This is a real poor man's salad, as the dandelions can be plucked along the hedges and byways and the cress from the running brook. This is strictly herbal and a real health-giving salad. In the spring of the year there is no more healthful, economical, satisfying salad in the entire category of salads than this one . . ."

The Vicomte de Mauduit provides a similar model in his *Vicomte in the Kitchen*, demonstrating plants' invulnerability to our petty ideas about social class.

Dandelion Salad: In the spring, if out walking in the fields or over the golf links, take with you a small basket and a short kitchen knife. With the knife uproot the dandelions and collect them in your basket. On your return home wash the dandelion carefully, break the leaves apart, drain in a salad basket, then wipe them in a cloth. Put them in a salad bowl together with one cold boiled beetroot cut into thin slices. Make over this an oil and vinegar salad dressing, and mix until your arms are tired.

Aristocrats may have low tolerances for fatigue. It doesn't take long to dress a dandelion salad. Contrary to the Vicomte's advice, you should still have strength at the end. His recipe is otherwise irreproachable, except for the beetroot, which we call beet, whose inclusion is superfluous.

Byways and running brooks are becoming as rare and exclusive as membership in golf clubs, and dandelions and watercress can be expensive if you are a city dweller, especially as what is satisfying in such a salad is mostly aesthetic.

Here is a version I make in my proletarian town, boundaried not by hedges and brooks—or golf greens—but passenger train tracks at one end and cargo-train tracks at the other. It is especially satisfying eaten alongside a Rich Man's Dish.

HERB SALAD

2 cups fresh strong herbs, such as cilantro, fennel fronds,
    chamomile, anise hyssop, wood sorrel
1 cup fresh parsley leaves
1 tablespoon minced shallot (about ½ a shallot)
1 tablespoon lemon juice
¼ teaspoon kosher salt, plus a tiny sprinkle more to taste
olive oil

*Pick over the herb leaves and wash and dry them in small batches; put
them in a large bowl. Cover the shallot with lemon juice. Add a pinch
of salt and leave to sit for 10 minutes. Pour over the herbs and mix delicately with your hands. Add a long stream of olive oil and again mix
through. Taste and adjust the salt and oil, leaving it piquant and exciting. Serve immediately.*

There is ample room for improvisation. If there is only parsley
around, this can be a fine salad of it alone.

On the other hand, I am reminded of those menus left in the diary
of the sixteenth-century Florentine painter so well known for his
spectral perspective, the man known as Pontormo. The wild plant
borage features prominently in the frugal, depressed man's daily
rations. There is even a salad made from borage flowers, which are
light blue and beautiful. They taste of cucumber and still grow wild,
even in very harsh environs. It is worth keeping a lookout—and look
down—for them wherever you are.

(I add, digressively, that borage flowers make a good, if cloudy,
infusion of gin. They leave it tasting of herbal cucumber. It is delicious, but best served in soft light.) Wild nasturtium flowers, leaves,
and buds also make fine additions to salads, though odd-tasting gin.

A good salad of almost monkish probity is watercress salad. Like the
"Poor Man's Salad," this began as the true tramp's relish, free to anyone with passage to a stream. It doesn't as neatly fit the circumstance

of the uprooted urban citizen, but it makes up in simplicity and naturalness what it lacks in economy and creativity.

WATERCRESS SALAD

¼ to ½ lemon
2 cups watercress, thoroughly cleaned, thickest stems removed
2 tablespoons olive oil, or more to taste
kosher salt

Squeeze about one-quarter of the lemon over the watercress and mix lightly, then add the olive oil and salt. Taste, adding more lemon, salt, and olive oil as you like.

Anything left behind in the bowl after dinner makes a good addition to a sandwich the following day.

Treated as occasional relief to rich dishes that must be "main" but don't need a "side"—like grilled quails on canapés (page 177) and steak Diane hallelujah (page 184) and soufflés (pages 147 and 150), these small arrangements of bright-flavored leaves are neither garnish—a word too close to *garish* to ever trust—nor full partner. They are supportive, and counteract the occasional ponderous bite of a rich dish with their restorative faculties.

Almost all cookbooks, from the most elementary to the most connoisseurish, contain at least one recipe for the mixture known as classic vinaigrette. They are basically the same. The recipe is, however, often somewhat hidden, a) because you are encouraged to follow its instructions only when you make Fufu's famous Bibb lettuce and tomato salad; or b) because in trying to seem unique it insists on a combination of lime juice, grapefruit juice, and Champagne vinegar—which is hogwash, since any acidic juice or vinegar other than balsamic (which is its own thing) is probably good as long as it is in the right combination with other elements and the oil is not rancid and the salt is not iodized.

Neither such a vinaigrette's application to Fufu's favorite formula nor heady mixing of citrus juices matters as much as the procedure for making it, which is too old for precise citation: finely minced shallot or onion and, if used, garlic, need ten minutes or so sitting with salt and whatever acid and/or mustard you use. This step takes the edge off sharp ingredients. It is into this calmed mixture that oil should be incorporated. Once that's done, lettuce loves it, and it loves lettuce.

Other things that matter: Cracked or freshly ground black pepper should, to my mind, be added, if it is to be added, to a salad itself rather than to its dressing, especially one as simple as vinaigrette. Pepper seeps into and makes everything peppery. The finest point is also the coarsest: what really matters is good lettuce.

Salades vinaigrette once appeared on menus by variety of lettuce— as on the Ambassador Hotel's from 1933, which offered "Heart of Lettuce; Romaine; Chicory; Watercress; or Mixed Greens *à la Française*." To me this list is the song of songs. Its salads all rely on the monogamous agreement between lettuce leaves and classic vinaigrette, which is so singular, and so good to leave alone.

A plain green salad vinaigrette is delicious with the Ambassador's selections. If, however, you live near a farm where new farmers tend old seeds, like Lolla Rossa or Merveille de Quatre Saisons or Speckled or Three Heart or Tennis Ball, or any of hundreds of others, they may be even better.

A PLAIN GREEN SALAD VINAIGRETTE

2 tablespoons finely diced spring onion or shallot
kosher salt
juice of 1 lemon
1 tablespoon smooth Dijon mustard
5 to 6 tablespoons olive oil, or more as needed
1 head soft lettuce, leaves removed at the base with a sharp
        knife, dunked in cold water to clean, spun in batches until
        almost dry, and left to dry on a large cloth napkin

Make the vinaigrette by combining the onion, salt, and lemon juice in a small bowl. Leave to macerate for 10 minutes. Add the mustard. Mix through, then add the olive oil, mixing well with a spoon or whisk. Taste it on a leaf and add more olive oil or salt until you like it. Season the lettuce alone with a tiny bit of salt, then drizzle with the vinaigrette, stopping shy of all of it. Mix through gently with your hands. Add more vinaigrette, if you like.

A handful of salted cucumber slices or sliced roasted beets, dressed in red wine vinegar and olive oil, can be added. These suggest a kind of intrusive polygamy. But my *Permaculture Guide to Companion Planting* assures me that they grow well alongside lettuce in the garden, apparently to mutual benefit. Either should be arranged discretely among lettuce leaves after the leaves have gotten dressed.

On certain occasions—which? A full moon? Winter, certainly, when good head lettuce is hard to come by—an equally satisfying version can be made with the white, tapered leaves of the Belgian endive. The slightly bitter, long, firm petals, so often subjected to walnuts and apples, make a pale, elegant salad, alone or with parsley leaves, dressed with plain vinaigrette. Or, easier, if it is winter and endive is hard to find, is celery, which stays crisp despite a crisper's best efforts to wilt it, or fennel, sliced into paper-thin wings. Or cooled cooked broccoli cut into thin slices, or cooked winter squash, or potatoes, or sweet potatoes, or turnips, any of which can be turned into a classic salad vinaigrette.

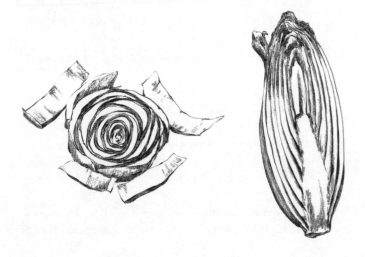

A less classic salad can be made with the thick herbal dressing possessing the pompous name Green Goddess. Green Goddess dressing was first served at the Palace Hotel in San Francisco in 1923. It was devised in honor of a play by the same name, a relic featuring the Rajah of Rukh, his valet, the good Doctor Basil Traherne—a fittingly herbal name—and a wife named Lucilla in tailor-made tweeds, and set in "a remote region at the back of the Himalayas."

GREEN GODDESS SALAD

1 egg yolk, at room temperature
⅛ teaspoon smooth Dijon mustard
¾ to 1 cup olive oil
6 tablespoons chopped mixed fresh parsley, tarragon, and chives
3 anchovy fillets, chopped
½ small clove garlic, pounded to a paste with a tiny bit of salt
1½ to 2 tablespoons white wine vinegar
kosher salt
1 head Italian chicory, or a few heads Belgian endive, or, if you
    do not like bitter lettuces, a head of iceberg lettuce

Combine the egg yolk and mustard in a bowl. Very slowly whisk in the olive oil, drop by drop, until an emulsion has formed. Add drops of room-temperature water once the mixture becomes thick. When you have a good-tasting, slightly loose mayonnaise, add the herbs. Mash the anchovies with the garlic paste and add them to the mayonnaise. Whisk in the vinegar, tasting it on a leaf and adjusting the vinegar and salt. Toss the chicory with the dressing, drizzling it to the side of the bowl, adding only as much as you like.

A friend adds avocado and calls the solution "debased." I reject the deprecation—half an avocado contributes both verdancy and a richness that might even be called *divine*, and surely only serves to enhance the affair. If I were following his habit, I would include avocado with the mustard and egg and then proceed. In either form, Green Goddess is tantalizing spooned over a wedge of the hardwearing crisp head known as iceberg—a name I like because, in the unintentional poetry of a yogic woman in my quiet town, it "sounds like it means."

This perhaps depraved practice can be refined if you drizzle the sturdy leaves first with lemon juice, then lightly salt them, and roll each wedge quickly with a little dressing in a mixing bowl, before pouring an agreeable dollop over each on its plate. This trick makes things seem more combined.

If you like iceberg but dislike buying lettuce from large companies, it is worth noting that a number of small farms, not named Foxy, have begun to grow the variety as smaller, less compact and industrial heads.

No soul can hear the words *buttermilk dressing* and not imagine a simpler time. Even if one has never tasted the dreamy concoction, it evokes making hay and milking cows and churning butter, then refreshment with cold glasses of revitalizing buttermilk. There must be a joyous main dish to accompany such nostalgic delight, the table laid with cold fried chicken on a worn tin platter, Grandma's German potato salad, and crisp greens, tossed at the last possible instant with . . .

BUTTERMILK DRESSING

3 tablespoons buttermilk
2 tablespoons full-fat plain Greek yogurt
1 small clove garlic, pounded to a paste with a little salt
½ teaspoon sugar
1 teaspoon minced shallot
1 teaspoon white wine vinegar
kosher salt
1 tablespoon olive oil
2 teaspoons finely chopped mixed fresh herbs (parsley, chives,
    chervil, or tarragon)
freshly ground black pepper

In a blender, combine the buttermilk, yogurt, garlic paste, and sugar. In a separate bowl, combine the shallot and vinegar with a tiny pinch of salt and let sit for 10 minutes. Add the buttermilk mixture to the shallot and whisk in the olive oil by hand. Add the herbs and some black pepper. Adjust the salt to taste.

The greens can be romaine or chicory or frisée—which makes an especially pretty buttermilk-shrouded tangle. Or they can be the crispest cucumbers, sliced and salted for fifteen minutes while the dressing's flavors are blending, then pressed dry and bathed in it. Or they can be neither green nor crisp: ripe summer tomatoes are very happy sliced and plattered with a jar of buttermilk dressing alongside. These provide a sense of overall well-being, no matter how complicated the times.

Blue cheese dressing is still served at pubs and steak houses, whether of the billionaire or LongHorn varieties, or the old-new copper kind. For all their differences, the three seem to agree on one recipe: a somewhat unwholesome and likable mixture of mayonnaise, sour cream, and blue cheese.

Here is another version. It is a marriage of the earliest blue cheese dressing recipe I have read, from Marion H. Neil's 1916 *Salads, Sand-*

wiches and Chafing Dish Recipes and one I tasted at Manhattan's La Mangeoire. La Mangeoire's salad is made with thin wedges of Belgian endive, which is both practical and elegant. The whole gives an impression of artful ease. Iceberg is also good, and Italian chicories, like sugarloaf and radicchio, which combine the best attributes of endive and iceberg—bitterness and crispness—make consummate partners. Combined with any, this dressing offers charm and simplicity and the irresistible contrast of fat, crisp, and cool.

BLUE CHEESE SALAD

½ cup chopped mixed fresh parsley, tarragon, chervil, dill, or
    chives (any combination)
1 cup homemade mayonnaise (see page 171)
optional: 1 small clove garlic
kosher salt
a few heads Belgian endive, or 1 head iceberg lettuce or Italian
    chicory
good olive oil, for drizzling
8 ounces Roquefort or Gorgonzola Dolce cheese, put in the
    freezer for 20 minutes
freshly ground black pepper

Mix the herbs into the mayonnaise. If using the garlic clove, pound it to a paste with a touch of salt and add it. Taste the dressing and adjust for salt. Toss wedges of endive lightly with olive oil and a little salt in a bowl. Arrange on plates. Dollop heavily with the herbed mayonnaise. Using a Microplane or the fine holes of a box grater, top each plate heavily with a mountain of Roquefort. Finish with freshly ground black pepper.

Another good variation on blue cheese dressing is to mix sour cream or straight heavy cream or crème fraîche with about half as much olive oil and a long drizzle of vinegar—white wine or red—then the amount of blue cheese you like, with or without garlic.

Green Goddess and buttermilk and blue cheese dressings also make pleasant sauces into which to dip vegetables, like carrots and radishes (and probably a thousand others), that ask to be eaten but, like naked babies, resist being dressed. They are also—of course—good beside fried oysters, fried green tomatoes, boiled potatoes, and, and, and.

Late last century, versions of French *salades composées*, or composed salads—distinct for not being "tossed" (an odd, terrible word for what is really a light-handed mixing) became popular main courses. These helped the category *Salad* formally transition from accompaniment to lobster Newburg or baked stuffed haddock to lunch.

The best-known French composed salads—*salade Niçoise* and *salade Lyonnaise*—do not only not need updates but suffer at their hands. *Salade Niçoise*, often topped today with bland, blackened rare tuna is better as it was conceived, with canned olive oil–packed tuna, best caught on long lines by smoking Spaniards. Lyonnaise was, is, and should be frisée, bacon lardons, and just-poached eggs.

Chef's salad is a different matter. It is an American *salade composée*. Like all things American, it was not ever made one way, then loyally repeated, but nearly constantly innovated on.

We do not know the original: the template of a composed salad of many elements goes back at least to sixteenth-century salmagundis, and there have been hundreds of variations since. What we know today as chef's salad was popularized by Louis Diat at New York's Ritz-Carlton in the 1940s and published in Diat's *Cooking à la Ritz* in 1941.

I provide his basic formula, which is not beautifully written, but admirable for its economy of prose and ingredients:

> Place separately in a salad bowl equal amounts of chopped lettuce (place on the bottom of the bowl), boiled chicken, smoked ox tongue and smoked ham, all cut in julienne style. Add one-half hard-cooked egg for each portion. Place some watercress in the center and serve with French dressing.

This is an obviously irreproachably conceived dish. It is composed of meat, greens, and eggs—and the last only appears as a chary single half apiece. Just as vital is that the meats are all slow cooked and chilled. This creates a different effect than their late-century replacements of reconstituted ham and turkey.

I have tried to preserve Diat's economies in my version.

HOME COOK'S SALAD

Boil the eggs according to the directions on page 14. Wash and dry frisée or radicchio or dandelion greens or watercress. Slice chilled braised meat, like leftover beef from beef bouilli (page 185), or pork from garbure (page 192), or the meat from chicken legs or thighs left over from poached chicken mayonnaise (page 170). Drizzle the meat with vinaigrette (page 77). Dress the greens with the same vinaigrette, lay them in a bowl or plate, and arrange the dressed meat on top, as you like. Halve the eggs and place two halves per person over the greens, salting them lightly and drizzling with more vinaigrette. If you have an herb, like parsley or cilantro or chives or dill, scatter some, roughly chopped, over everything.

This will feed as many eaters as you have and can as easily be made for one. The combination of chilled braised meat, sharp greens, and egg is such a pleasant and natural one that it makes sense to let it follow whatever natural unfurling occurs. The eggs may be poached, à la Lyonnaise. A ribbon or two of prosciutto may top it all, bringing you closer to M. Diat. I also recognize the almost therapeutic quality to sometimes putting everything you like into a single chilled bowl. Why shouldn't your version of this protean salad feature chilled wild shrimp, or grilled tiny squid, making it marine? The first known printed recipe for chef's salad, from the 1936 *Joy of Cooking*, contained sliced radishes and anchovies. These are good additions, and themselves suggest others—capers might be scattered over eggs. Pretty multicolored watermelon radishes are uniquely lovely sliced and laid about in shingles. To nod to the Thousand Island dressing that eventually took the place of Diat's demur vinaigrette, you might include judicious blobs of homemade garlic mayonnaise, to which you are welcome to add ketchup if that is your taste.

If you like your chef's salad to be a farrago of eggs and ham and turkey and cheese, claim your farrago. Dress each element on its own, since dressing any ingredient in a crowd ends with something over-dressed and something inexplicably naked. And give each category its own pretty section of the plate so that the farrago is thoughtfully composed.

A main-dish salad from even earlier is crab Louis. There is a great deal of good to say about this salad, which surely sprang fully formed, like Athena from Zeus's skull, from the misty docks along Washington State or Oregon or Northern California's foggy coast where Dungeness crab swim thick. A crab Louis recipe from the 1910 cookbook of Victor Hirtzler, the chef at San Francisco's St. Francis Hotel, is vivid if, like Louis Diat's recipe, almost too terse.

Crab salad, Louis. Arrange lettuce leaves around the inside of a salad bowl, with a few sliced leaves on the bottom. Put crab meat on top of the sliced leaves, and a few sliced hard boiled eggs and sliced chives on top of the crab meat. In another bowl mix one-half cup of French dressing with one-half cup of Chili sauce, two spoonfuls of mayonnaise, salt, pepper, and one teaspoonful of Worcestershire sauce. Pour over the salad, and serve very cold.

As is custom—or perhaps rule—with iconic dishes, fanatics claim it for their city or region. San Francisco's Palace Hotel asserts ownership of the much copied salad. So does the Davenport in Oregon. With such disputes comes a natural suspicion that no version is right. In *American Cookery*, James Beard wrote: "I don't think anyone is certain of the recipe for the original crab Louis, of which there have been many different and many horrible versions." Beard offers as consolation this dressing recipe, for which he appears to vouch, from the Bohemian restaurant in Portland, Oregon, where "Louis was served during its heyday: Combine 1 cup mayonnaise with ⅓ cup whipped cream, ⅓ cup chili sauce, 1 tablespoon grated onion, and a touch of cayenne." (High Americana!) I'm sure there was an honesty and even subtlety to Beard's version when he wrote and prepared it. But it seems to me to too much disguise the delicate purity of crab and lettuce.

I like this longer recipe. I know that mine cannot be called crab Louis, having been told so by people whose tempers I've inflamed. The salad on which it is based already shares a first name with one of my favorite people. So my illicit version also shares his second name. I call it . . .

CRAB LOUIS DASHIELL

3 or 4 heads Little Gem lettuce, 2 heads Boston lettuce, or 1
    head iceberg lettuce
1 English cucumber, peeled, halved lengthwise, and seeded
¼ teaspoon kosher salt, plus more as needed
3 tablespoons sherry or distilled white vinegar
5 eggs, at room temperature
¼ teaspoon smooth Dijon mustard
1 tablespoon fresh lemon juice, plus to taste
1 cup not-sharp, good-tasting olive oil
1 stalk green garlic, white and light green parts, or ½ clove
    regular garlic, pounded to a paste with a little salt
2½ tablespoons finely chopped cucumber pickles
1 tablespoon finely chopped shallot
1½ teaspoons chopped drained capers
3 tablespoons drained prepared horseradish
1 pound picked-through jumbo lump crabmeat (canned is fine),
    chilled
hot sauce
optional: flaky salt
fresh chives, chopped, or chive blossoms

*Wash the lettuce and dry it in a salad spinner and on dishtowels. Chill.
Cut the cucumber into bite-size pieces. Sprinkle with the salt and the
sherry, and leave to marinate. Cook, peel, and halve 4 of the eggs as
for deviled eggs (see page 16). With the remaining egg, mustard, lemon
juice, and olive oil, make mayonnaise as on page 171. Add the garlic,
chopped pickles, shallot, capers, and horseradish. Mix well and taste for
salt. Refrigerate, covered, if not using immediately. Arrange the lettuce
on plates. Drain and divide the cucumbers among them. Add the eggs,
salting each lightly. Divide the crab among the salads. Shake hot sauce
directly over the crab on each plate. Dollop each salad with dressing,
mostly on the crab. Finish with flaky salt, if using, and chopped chives
or chive blossoms. Eat cold.*

To my mind the best restaurant version of crab Louis is found at Swan Oyster Depot in San Francisco, where the dressing's hue nears the deep coral of a Polynesian sunset. To give the mixture this voluptuous complexion, add chile sauce.

Swan's salad is strict: crab, lettuce, sauce, *fin*. But there is sense and even amusement to exuberant additions of fat green asparagus, quickly boiled in very salty water, or ripe avocado, or little sweet cherry tomatoes, halved and salted, or boiled new potatoes . . . These corruptions bring the added benefit of requiring less crab per person, which, unless you live along the same misty docks whence the salad first came, is good news for the budget conscious. Simply add what you like and pay attention to whether you like it, in the end. This salad is named after my son, a delicate mixture of ingredients known and unknown—to us, and even to himself—all of which I love more than I ever could have guessed.

A different matter again is the recognizable and sustaining Waldorf. This salad took firm hold at the turn of the century, when the sacrosanct light of domestic science shone on everything in the kitchen, and to be considered modern, a salad had to be bound—with mayonnaise or sour cream or Jell-O.

Waldorf salad was a fixture at "nice ladies' luncheons" in the 1950s. The nice ladies I know would almost certainly have peered bleakly at the tame concoction and ordered in its place a dry gin and rare beef. If, however, they had been served the salad in its earliest days, things might have gone differently. Like the chef's salad, the Waldorf in its original form was tasteful: a synchronous alignment of things that eventually, as ingredients and ideas were added, fell out of tune. It was at first made of apples, celery, and mayonnaise, which are, on a more atomic level, apples, celery, egg, olive oil, mustard, and lemon. The constituent parts, pared thin and crisp, dressed and combined, are refreshing and plain. The result is a salad that is at the same time substantial and almost luminously delicate. This Waldorf salad brings a rare double happiness: some of what was good about a dish for which we have developed institutional distaste, and a new version that tastes current.

WALDORF SALAD, IN PIECES

2 tablespoons fresh lemon juice
½ teaspoon smooth Dijon mustard
kosher salt
¼ cup olive oil, plus to taste
2 large stalks celery, thinly sliced on an angle (2 cups)
1 fresh crisp apple, thinly sliced (I like RubyFrost or Mutsu, not
    Granny Smith, which are too sour, and nothing too Red
    or Delicious . . .)
3 eggs, cooked according to the directions for deviled eggs (see
    page 16) and quartered
optional: flaky salt, for finishing

Whisk 1 tablespoon of the lemon juice with the mustard, a pinch of salt, and the olive oil and dress the celery with this, rubbing it through with your hands. Let sit for 10 minutes. Sprinkle the apple with the remaining 1 tablespoon lemon juice, then combine with the celery, again mixing with your hands. Spread into a thick rough layer on a platter and position the egg wedges here and there. Sprinkle the eggs with salt. Drizzle with olive oil, and finish with flaky salt, if you like.

If the procedure of dressing first the celery, then the apple makes you impatient, dress them together. The result will be less subtle but not worse. If you like more texture and more heartiness, the addition of walnuts to the old Waldorf—perhaps, the story goes, by a chef whose family had a walnut tree—offers itself up. So does an addition of crumbled Roquefort cheese or Gorgonzola Dolce—which can be adopted with impunity as long as you do the crumbling yourself, as pre-crumbled versions tend to taste old and dusty.

Before any of those main dish salads were invented, named, stolen, or served, American salads that were not simply from the garden were made of leftover chicken—unless we were from Maine, where everything is "the way life should be," and used leftover lobster. This leftover salad, which is based on one by Rufus Estes in his 1911 *Good*

Things to Eat, can absorb any fowl, fish, or other finding. It is simple and appeals to the faintest and the firmest of appetites.

ANYTHING AND PICKLE SALAD

½ cup chopped cucumber pickles or dilly beans
1 cup chopped cooked meat, fish, eggs, or beans
1 tablespoon chopped fresh dill
⅛ teaspoon dried hot mustard
1½ teaspoons heavy cream
kosher salt and freshly ground black pepper
optional: a few drops of Tabasco

Combine everything in a bowl and mix together well with a large spoon, adding salt and lots of black pepper to taste. Add a few drops of Tabasco, if you like.

With the ends of a roast chicken, this is a "shortcut to thrift," and with lobster—or wild shrimp—it is a delicacy. In the second case I might use fewer pickles so the shrimp or lobster could shine through— or I might not, trusting the well-matched flora and fauna to collaborate.

A particularly delightful version can be made with cooked mussels. Then, you might add little new potatoes, boiled in their jackets and sliced and drizzled with a bit more heavy cream mixed with a dash of dried mustard, and more fresh dill over it all. Any variation is delicious as a sandwich, with a few additional slices of pickle if you like.

You might also serve it, if you are in a coy, backward-looking mood, in an alligator pear.

What is an alligator pear? Something familiar by a foreign name. It lived an abused if tolerable life until one bright morning under the Nixon administration when it awoke to learn it would no longer be harassed with salads of chicken or lobster or anything. It would be left to stand on its own. It would moreover be called . . . *avocado.*

I am happy for the dignifying. But it remains as true now as it ever was that if a ripe avocado is filled with a culinary echo of the bridal refrain of something old, something new . . . of something rich, something acid, something salty, something crisp, it is a small, correct opulence.

ALLIGATOR PEAR SALAD

1 ripe avocado
¼ teaspoon kosher salt, plus to taste
3 tablespoons finely chopped red onion
juice of ½ lemon
1 (4-ounce) can olive oil–packed tuna, with its oil
4 teaspoons roughly chopped toasted salted almonds
2 tablespoons roughly chopped fresh parsley
2 tablespoons very good olive oil
freshly ground black pepper

Halve the avocado lengthwise. Remove the pit and scoop out a very small amount of the flesh from the center of each half, leaving most of it attached to the avocado skin and reserving whatever you scoop out. Lightly salt the inside of the avocado. Soak the onion in the lemon juice with the ¼ teaspoon salt for 10 to 15 minutes. Add the avocado you've scooped, the tuna, almonds, parsley, olive oil, lots of black pepper, and more salt to taste. Mix it lightly to combine, leaving large chunks of the tuna and avocado. Fill the avocado halves with the mixture, mounding it up slightly. Save any extra for a sandwich.

This seemly dish is a small meal on its own (especially if you eat both halves, as I sometimes do). It is also a wonderful preamble to a second salad—a new practice that would have once been scorned—of freshly boiled tiny green beans and tomatoes with buttermilk or Green Goddess dressing, or Waldorf salad in pieces, or any unnamed combination of good vegetables, cooked or resolutely not, but only seasoned with salt and vinaigrette, as you like.

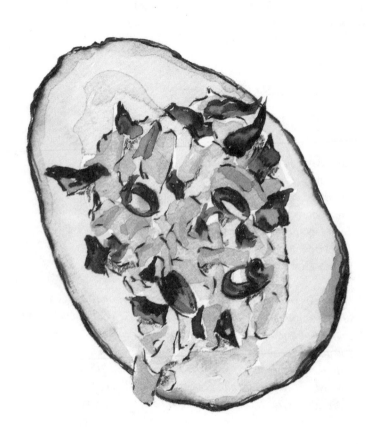

If that *is* what you like, you might dispense with the entire idea of stuffing the avocado and follow these instructions for a French bistro classic on which I survived for a week in Paris long ago:

> *Avocat en vinaigrette:* Cut the avocado in half lengthwise and remove the pit. Add classic vinaigrette to its middle, and add salt and pepper to taste.

If the spooning of a salad into an avocado appeals to you, sardines can be traded for tuna. Or cucumber, per *Good Things to Eat,* "chopped fine and squeezed dry, then seasoned with mayonnaise." Or chickpeas or lentils or feta cheese, *quantum sufficit.* Or why not stuff the little alligator pear with the salad of anything and pickles (page 90)? Or, come to think of it, why not with chopped leftover boiled eggs, sprinkled with herbs and lemon juice? Or brown rice? Such matches may not have the purity of vegetable love, but nor do our own amorous partnerships, and we continue to form them with optimism, if not always success.

Perhaps our partnerings would be more successful if we entrusted them to plants; if we listened to the opinionated Vicomte de Mauduit, preaching hoarily from his kitchen:

> It being said that succory [a wild chicory with cornflower blue flowers] ensures constancy in love, let us make a Succory Salad. Take the leaves, cut them small, put them in cold water for two hours, change the water three times and dry them. Mix them with slices of cooked beetroot, sprinkle some chopped samphire [sea beans], make over this a French salad dressing and mix all thoroughly.

Will our arms not tire from this mixing? Will we still have strength for loving embraces? The Vicomte believes so, and I trust him. We should sup on succory salad. And perhaps wake to find our loves as true, inviolable, and constant as a vegetable's.

A FANCY
SUMMER DINNER

Aubergines en hors d'œuvre

Wine: A bracing and bubbly rosé
Example: Rosé Champagne
Gatinois Brut Rosé NV

Grilled quails on canapés

Herbed tomatoes

Garlicky green beans amandine

Watercress salad

Wine: A fruity, spicy red with soft tannins
and juicy acidity
Example: Cru Beaujolais
Lapierre Morgon 2015

Plum cake

IN VEGETABLE VERITAS

Vegetables

IV

A turnip is not necessarily a depressant.
—*The Joy of Cooking*, 1943

"Who determines," M.F.K. Fisher once wrote, "and for what strange reasons, the social status of a vegetable?" And how do they ensure that what is yesterday's garden mulch is today's Mayday queen (and vice versa)? The turnip, cabbage, and carrot have long been treated as purely functional alternatives to hunger. Now they have risen, and that has meant other plants' fall.

Zucchini, which in the 1960s, as Craig Claiborne wrote, was "such a considerable oddity that it was necessary to define it among the ingredients as 'green Italian squash,'" is one casualty. The old disdain has set in, and the green Italian squash is (almost) necessarily a depressant.

When zucchini was exotic, its presence was uplifting, and it was treated as a treasure. One good example is a 1982 recipe cooked by Georges Blanc of La Mère Blanc, for "a gossamer, velutinous mousse of zucchini and leeks," under the name of *gâteau de courgettes*. These are a delicious adaptation of that gâteau.

GÂTEAUX DE COURGETTES

2 tablespoons butter, plus more for greasing
about ½ pound leeks, cut into half-moons and washed well (2
    very heaping cups)
1 tablespoon kosher salt, plus to taste

1½ pounds zucchini, chopped (4 to 5 cups)
big pinch of saffron threads
1 tablespoon chopped fresh dill or parsley, or 1 teaspoon dried
    Greek oregano
2 eggs, separated
4½ tablespoons crème fraîche
a little grated Parmesan cheese, for dusting
1 egg white

Heat the oven to 275 degrees. Put a pan large enough to hold your cups or ramekins on the middle rack and pour in a few inches of hot water. Melt the butter in a large shallow pan over medium heat. Add the leeks and ½ tablespoon of the salt. Cook until tender, 2 to 3 minutes, then add the zucchini and remaining ½ tablespoon salt. Cook over medium heat, stirring often, until completely tender, adding sprinkles of room-temperature water as needed to keep the zucchini from burning. Add the saffron and mix through while the pan is still warm. Add the herbs.

Purée the vegetables in a food processor. Once smooth, add the egg yolks and crème fraîche. Taste for salt: it should be slightly overseasoned.

Butter six oven-safe cups or ramekins. Coat the insides lightly with grated Parmesan, tapping out the excess.

Whip the egg whites to just past soft peaks, stopping while they are still shiny. Whisk one-third of the whipped egg whites into the vegetable-yolk mixture to lighten it. Add the rest and distribute among the prepared cups or ramekins. Set the cups or ramekins into the hot water bath and bake until just firm, 45 to 55 minutes. Remove from the ramekins by running a knife around their insides and upending them onto plates.

This quivering little pudding is a perfect accompaniment to a plain main course, like wild salmon, or a chicken paillard, hammered paper-thin, well seasoned with salt, and cooked quickly in butter and olive oil. Georges Blanc served a fish course and lamb with his gâteau, a small but not dangerous excess.

Here is a variation on the old chestnut, stuffed zucchini. It is lighter than the originals—full of herbs, sweet onions, and the insides of the zucchini, which were in the past often discarded. It is best with tiny zucchini and as a result takes longer than is sensible for getting a dish's pieces in order. But the stuffing is a perfect occupation for the idle hands of guests otherwise occupied with only glasses of Champagne.

STUFFED ZUCCHINI

3 to 4 tablespoons olive oil, plus more for greasing
kosher salt
2 to 3 pounds very small zucchini
2 tablespoons butter
2 cloves garlic
1 large Torpedo onion, or ½ white onion, finely chopped
8 or 9 large whole anchovy fillets
a small pinch chile flakes
⅓ cup chopped mixed fresh herbs (basil, marjoram, rosemary, thyme, parsley, dill)
1½ cups grated Parmesan cheese
freshly ground black pepper

Heat the oven to 400 degrees. Oil the bottom of a large roasting dish. Bring a big pot of water to a boil. Salt it to taste like seawater. Cut the zucchini into 1- to 2-inch pieces. With a little spoon, dig out the insides, leaving ¼ inch on the sides and bottom of each. If the zucchini is too thin, scoop it out lengthwise like a boat. Finely chop the flesh you removed from inside the zucchini and set aside. Cook the empty zucchini in the boiling water (at or near a boil) for 30 seconds to 1 minute, in two or three batches. Remove to the waiting baking dish with a slotted spoon. Continue until all the zucchini are cooked.

Heat a large sauté pan. Add the olive oil and butter, then the garlic, onion, and a small pinch of salt. When the onion has begun to soften, add the anchovies and chile flakes, breaking up the anchovies as you stir. Once the onion has begun to look translucent, add the reserved zucchini. Cook, stirring occasionally, until softened and beginning to fry. Turn off the heat and add the herbs. Remove to a bowl, add 1 cup of the Parmesan and freshly ground black pepper to taste. Taste for salt and adjust.

Turn the zucchini in the baking dish with the to-be-stuffed side up.

Stuff, distributing the filling evenly. Sprinkle evenly with the remaining ½ cup Parmesan, then drizzle with olive oil.

Bake, uncovered, on the top rack, close to the heat, for 30 minutes, or until starting to brown on top.

The delicate result of this extractive to-do is uniquely good with *steak haché* (page 182), or for something simpler, sliced tomatoes, a wedge of strong cheese, and thick, garlic-rubbed toast.

Here is a final zucchini dish, which I hope will give the vegetable the leg back up it needs. It is a variation on the theme of stewed vegetables from before the insistence that all vegetables be cooked only until al dente. Zucchini is delightful cooked until collapsed. This is best kept for that moment in late summer when zucchini is very fat and sweet.

BUTTERED ZUCCHINI

4 or 5 medium zucchini
4 tablespoons olive oil
2 tablespoons unsalted butter
2 cloves fresh or 1 clove cured garlic
1 whole Torpedo onion, or ½ white onion
kosher salt
2 fresh or 1 dried chile, whole
½ cup whole fresh basil leaves
1 tablespoon heavy cream
½ cup chopped fresh dill or 3 tablespoons dried oregano
freshly ground black pepper

I like to cut the zucchini in this strange way: Cut all the curved sides off the zucchini, so they are rectangular. Cut the insides into cubes, about ½ inch around, and slice the skin into matchsticks. This gives things a wonderful texture. (Or just quarter the zucchini lengthwise and then cut crosswise into ½-inch pieces.)

Heat 2 tablespoons of the olive oil and the butter in a deep pot. Add the garlic and onion and a big pinch of salt. Cook over low heat, stirring, for 1 to 2 minutes. Add the zucchini, chiles, and half the basil leaves and cover. Cook over low heat for about 15 minutes, opening up to check and stir once or twice.

Uncover and cook, adjusting the heat as you like, covering and uncovering, until the zucchini begins to sizzle and lose a bit of its liquid, but still has some. Add the remaining 2 tablespoons olive oil and stir vigorously so the zucchini fries a bit. Season with salt and continue to cook and stir until it tastes good. Over high heat, add the cream and cook, stirring, until it's fully integrated. Turn off the heat. Add the rest of the herbs and a lot of black pepper. Serve hot or room temperature. This is very good served with crisp brown toast.

If you smooth the zucchini into a buttered gratin dish and sizzle it under the broiler for a minute until its top is bubbling and browned, it will look more self-possessed, but this clinically correct step seems gratuitous to me. The dish is rugged and right as is. For the rest of the meal, one needs only something basic like steamed clams or scrambled eggs.

The same recipe can be made with romano beans, or tough, end-of-season green beans. It certainly also works with other vegetables I haven't thought of or don't know. I am blindered in my perspective, as much as anyone who has grown up subtly unconscious of why certain foods are treats and others punishments.

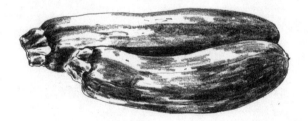

Once, before its name was vitiated by the French Nazi government, Vichy, France, was known for its waters, for the men and women who took steam engine trains to its stone baths, deep in the Bourbonnais, and for carrots cooked in curative water, butter, and sugar, called *carottes Vichy.*

Carrots Vichy, even if updated with a dozen new tricks, like substituting maple syrup or honey for sugar, or adding paprika or parsley, are cloyingly sweet. My alternative—too elementary for the virtuous instruction of a recipe—ends in a surprising composition, elegant enough in flavor for the once graceful name . . . *Vichy.*

Bring a large pot of water containing a little bundle of thyme and parsley stems to boil. Peel a bunch of big, sweet carrots. Cut each into oblique shapes by slicing a piece off on an angle, rotating the carrot 90 degrees, then cutting on the same angle again and repeating until the end. Salt the water to taste like seawater and cook in two batches, tasting after 3 to 4 minutes for doneness and removing them with a handheld sieve to a waiting platter. Discard the herbs. Drizzle the carrots heavily with good olive oil. These are truly delicious.

You can do the same with the little white turnips called Tokyo, leaving their green tops attached, quartering the larger and halving the smaller, and submerging only their bulbs in boiling water until the last few moments, during which their tops, too, should take a 10-second-long dip. These should be heavily oiled with the best olive oil you can find the instant they're out of the water.

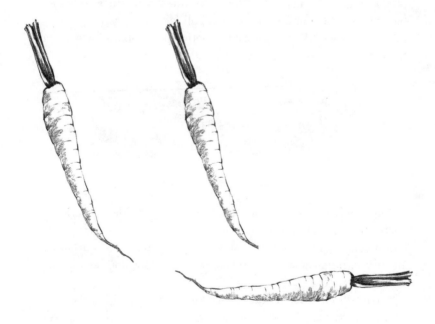

Neither is *Vichy* at all. But both depend on water, as did the fame of the town with the stone baths. Such carrots or turnips (or cauliflower or broccoli florets, or snap peas, or thin green beans, treated the same way) might simply be referred to, due to the almost-seawater in which they briefly bob, as vegetables *à la mer.*

The same turnips make a magnificent gratin. Or should I somewhat obstinately call such a preparation "scalloped turnips," with a tedious desire to teach what I have learned?

The scalloped dishes of the two centuries before today were either thinly sliced vegetable or meat or fowl, cooked in some way, *or* creamy dishes that were once baked in a scallop shell. If these sound very like a gratin, perhaps of potato, or cauliflower, or even turnip, you tasted years ago at an almost forgotten lunch at Great-Aunt Hokeypokes's house that you knew instinctively was good, it is because scalloped dishes *were* all gratins. *Gratin* means only that the top of a dish is browned— it will often contain thinly sliced meat or vegetables because they look pretty cut into pieces and cook well that way. Before the great (and we now know misguided) alarm was sounded toward the end of last century, warning everyone but Great-Aunt Hokeypokes away from good fats like cream, butter, and cheese, gratins were ubiquitous. In our time, as the fog of misinformation about dietary fat clears, they are a rare pleasure.

My preference is for this one of turnips, an uncommon dish in an uncommon field. I find everything about it encouraging.

TURNIP GRATIN

2 pounds Tokyo turnips, or other good sweet turnips, like
      Purple Tops, greens removed and cooked for another
      meal
½ cup chicken stock
¾ cup heavy cream
butter
kosher salt
4 sprigs thyme, leaves roughly stripped off

2 cloves garlic, very thinly sliced
optional: freshly ground black pepper
2 cups freshly grated Gruyère or Comté cheese

Heat the oven to 375 degrees. Thinly slice the turnips ⅛ to ¹/₁₆ inch thick on a mandoline or using expert fastidiousness and a knife. Reserve the prettiest slices for the top and conceal the uneven ones in early layers, where they will never be seen. Bring the stock and half the cream to a low simmer. Butter a 9-by-13(ish)-inch roasting pan or gratin dish. Layer the turnip slices, slightly overlapping them, lightly salt, speckle with thyme leaves, a few slices of garlic, and black pepper if you like, then ladle the warm cream-stock mixture over to just barely cover. Lightly strew with cheese. Continue this layering until all the turnip slices have been used up. Add enough liquid, using the rest of the cream if needed, to just barely cover the top layer, then cover it heavily with cheese. Cover with aluminum foil and bake for 45 minutes to 1 hour, until a knife inserted into the gratin goes through very easily. Turn the oven temperature up to 425 degrees, uncover, and bake for 15 to 20 minutes more, until all liquid has evaporated and the cheese on top is melted and browned. Top with freshly ground black pepper. Let cool for 15 minutes, then serve.

A friend, a fine classic cook, has typed to me, with a pungency that can almost be scented, that his turnip gratin is made of "béchamel, preferably with ham in it (and onion stuck with a clove, bay, then removed), no other meat or cheese, breadcrumbs and butter on top." I am persuaded and recommend his, too, believing it both delicious and comme il faut.

It is not at all a vegetable, though, per my juvenile logic, green like one, so this gratin, directly from *Larousse Gastronomique*, must be supplied:

Gratin Savoyard of frogs' legs: Allow 12 pairs of frogs' legs per person. Trim them, season with salt and pepper, dip in milk and then lightly in flour. Fry in butter with shallots and a little chopped garlic, then drain and arrange them in a fairly large baking dish. Dilute the pan juices with Mandement wine or with a fruity white wine; reduce and pour over the frogs' legs. Sprinkle with chopped chives and parsley, then squeeze the juice of a lemon over them. Mix together 1 cup heavy cream, ¾ cup grated Gruyère, and 2 egg yolks. Season with salt and pepper and pour over the frogs' legs. Brown under the broiler and serve garnished with a few fluted slices of lemon.

It is a short step from carrots and turnips and their perceived banality to potatoes as a ho-hum gastronomic cliché. Potato snubbing is justified in the view of a certain kind of gourmet rationalist, who has conviction that inexpensive spuds should become inexpensive dishes—potatoes, in other words, are cheap and should stay that way. My view is contradictory. The humble potato deserves special doting on *because* it is cheap, and because it is so good at absorbing any herb or fat it is offered.

Both of us can be satisfied by a classic potato dish known as parsleyed potatoes, which was inescapable at the middle of last century. Parsleyed potatoes are economical and elegant, and can be done different ways. Through trial and error, I've developed two techniques and one true *recipe*, though even its method is almost too casual a scheme for the format.

The first is to cook little new potatoes whole, in water as salty as the Dead Sea, starting them in cold water, bringing the water to a fast boil, then lowering it to below a simmer and cooking like this until the potatoes are done. Holding a kitchen towel in one hand, quickly rub or peel the skins from the potatoes while they are still very hot, your fingers shielded by cloth, and drop them into a bowl containing finely chopped parsley and several tablespoons of butter. The potato flesh, thirsty as a desert, will soak up the butter and parsley as parched earth does rain.

Or put the empty pot back over low heat, add the drained potatoes, skins on, add parsley and butter, and shake them vigorously back and forth. This is faster and easier on the fingers, but the butter and parsley don't make as definitive an impression on the potatoes.

This last is the most rustic. It produces my favorite of the three, if the least classic.

PARSLEYED POTATOES

2 pounds small waxy potatoes
1 small clove garlic, chopped
kosher salt
leaves from 1 bunch parsley, chopped
olive oil

Boil the potatoes according to the directions on page 107. Meanwhile, pound the garlic to a paste with a little salt in a large mortar and pestle or on a cutting board. Add the parsley and pound into a dark green paste. Add olive oil to cover, then a bit more to make it a touch swimmy and saucy. Taste for salt and adjust. It should be utterly delicious.

Once the potatoes are done, remove them and cut them, while still hot, in rough halves. Put them into a large bowl and mix liberally with the garlic-parsley oil, adding as much as you like. Save whatever parsley oil you don't use for dolloping or drizzling elsewhere.

According to the Vicomte de Mauduit, Napoleon loved potatoes. "Never a meal would he partake of unless two, if not three, kinds of potatoes were on the menu." (This was, the Vicomte added, somewhat unkindly, to the unhappiness of Josephine, who tended sharply to her Empire figure.) *Cooked how?* one wonders. There would have been French fries, and the difficult and worth-it twice-fried *pommes soufflés*, and the more difficult shallow-fried *pommes Anna*. At least a century after Napoleon's death those were probably the most popular French (and so American) preparations. They are moreover all good. If you are all right with something more homespun, this next recipe is a fried potato recipe to have and hold. It leaves new potatoes in their gold or pink skins, smelling and tasting of the earth reborn.

FRIED POTATOES

2 pounds small, even-size potatoes
kosher salt
1 clove garlic, unpeeled
1 bay leaf
olive oil or duck or goose fat as needed
optional: flaky salt
1 lemon, wedged

Cook the potatoes according to the directions on page 107, including a clove of garlic and bay leaf in their cooking water. When just cool enough to touch, press each potato flat with the heel of your hand so it breaks. Drizzle with olive oil.

Warm ¼ inch of olive oil in a heavy pan until a speck of flour or a breadcrumb sizzles when dropped into it. Fry the flattened potatoes in batches for about 2 minutes per side, until crisp, removing them with a slotted spoon to a platter. Serve immediately, topped with flaky salt, if you like, and accompanied by lemon. Or, if the idea of hurrying to the table obviates the refreshment of gathering around one, keep them warm in a 200-degree oven. It will cost you crispness but earn you calm.

If your potatoes are larger, or you are feeling rushed, instead of pressing the potatoes to flatten them, halve them and fry them, cut side down, in the hot fat.

A bowl of these will make purchased pâté, as long as it is cool and served with crisp-crusted bread, into a meal. They are also a supremely festive accompaniment to hamburgers or *steak haché* (page 182).

Perhaps the most successful application of a basic formula once administered to all vegetables is potatoes Delmonico. The formula fits easily into prose. It is *Vegetable, Well Cooked*, mixed with *Cream*, dabbed with *Butter*, covered with *Breadcrumbs* or *Cheese* or both, *Broiled*.

There are a number of reasons this formula is not in itself bad— and worth keeping, defects aside. It's homely, but I like it. A spoonful of such a rich, voluptuously browned concoction will restore the frailest body. And if your vegetable is starchy, because it is old or by intrinsic design, cooking and cream and butter will improve it.

A bubbling gratin of potatoes, cream, and cheese, potatoes Delmonico was, as far as we know, first made by Charles Ranhofer, the first chef of Delmonico's, the first real restaurant in New York. The primary nature of the arrangement shines through. The recipe was published in 1894 in Ranhofer's 1,183-page tome *The Epicurean*. Versions of both dish and formula self-propagated and sprouted in diverse soils, each adapted to its environment. In *The Fannie Farmer Cookbook*, potatoes Delmonico are a third-generation leftovers arrangement, admirable in their economy if not delicacy. In *Taste of Home*, they are made with cheddar.

Here is the original recipe, updated by the current chef of Delmonico's, where one can still eat them beneath crystal chandeliers and the watchful eyes and prodigious breasts of a nineteenth-century fresco.

POTATOES DELMONICO

4 medium white potatoes
butter, for greasing
¾ cup whole milk
¼ cup heavy cream

½ teaspoon kosher salt
¼ teaspoon freshly ground white pepper
¼ teaspoon freshly grated nutmeg
2 tablespoons freshly grated Parmesan cheese

Wash (but do not peel) the potatoes, and quarter them lengthwise (so that, after cooking, they can be sliced into the longest strips possible). Bring 8 cups of water to a boil and add the potatoes. Boil for 10 minutes so that the potatoes are only partly cooked. Drain and let cool, then slice the potatoes into long strips.

Heat the oven to 425 degrees. Lightly butter a medium-size baking dish.

Mix the milk, cream, salt, white pepper, and nutmeg together in a bowl.

Heat a large frying pan over medium heat, then add the potatoes and cream mixture. Fold together well but gently, without mashing the potatoes, and cook for 10 minutes, lightly mixing occasionally so that they do not burn. Remove from the stove and fold in 1 tablespoon of the Parmesan.

Transfer the potatoes to the prepared baking dish and arrange evenly. Sprinkle with the remaining 1 tablespoon of Parmesan.

Place the uncovered baking dish into the upper-third of the oven, and bake for 6 minutes or until lightly browned.

Serve immediately.

A coarser but also good variation, for cabbage, comes from Marion Harland's 1873 *Common Sense in the Household: A Manual of Practical Housewifery*:

Ladies' Cabbage:

Boil a firm white cabbage fifteen minutes [!], changing the water then for more from the boiling tea-kettle. When tender, drain and set aside until perfectly cold. Chop fine, and add two beaten eggs, a tablespoonful of butter, pepper, salt, three tablespoonfuls rich milk or cream, Stir all well together, and bake in a buttered pudding-dish until brown. Eat very hot.

The exclamation point is mine. If cabbage boils for fifteen minutes— or more, for what other use has the fresh water from the teakettle?—it becomes cabbage mush. Four minutes suffice. The cabbage should, of course, be cut for cooking into thin wedges and the water salted copiously. Add 1 egg, not 2, and 3 tablespoons butter, not 1—melted so it can be mixed with the egg—and ½ cup soft breadcrumbs before the final bake (at 400 degrees for 20 to 30 minutes), and you have a redoubtable pick-me-up.

The same technique can be applied to cauliflower and endive, especially if the latter is, after its brief boil, well drained and wrapped in Bayonne ham or prosciutto, to excellent result.

Why Mrs. Harland called it "Ladies' Cabbage" I do not know. It was perhaps thought dainty . . . though it is as dainty as a moose in pointe shoes. Or perhaps because vegetables were considered nutritionally useless, ill food for the growing boy. I wonder if by karmic inversion vegetable-starved men got gout and rickets, while ladies, fed on cabbage and cream, grew secretly strong and hardy as plants.

If you have a cabbage that is not starchy at all, but straight from the garden, and you want to be able to more easily distinguish it from potatoes than the Ladies version permits, roast it.

Heat the oven to 400 degrees. Slice a firm cabbage in half, then into wedges through its core. Lay the wedges in single layers on two baking sheets. Drizzle both sides heavily with olive oil, and salt them twice as heavily as you think you should. Cook, checking and rotating the pans after 15 minutes, until the cabbage is completely tender and dark and blistered in places. Serve this egalitarian preparation, which may be called Everyone's Cabbage, with lemon wedges.

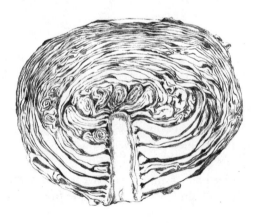

Cabbage in either guise shows an affinity for braised or poached meat, or sausages or scrambled eggs, and, so well proved by those crude, delicious, working-class dishes with tempting names—bubble and squeak and stamppot—boiled, buttered potatoes.

I often read vegetable recipes that follow Mrs. Harland et al's formula, wading through their eccentricities and cream without feeling at all compelled to stand up and begin chopping.

Three recipes simmered like this in my mind for years, letting me imagine the circumstances in which they would be cooked, without ever being moved to cook them. The first is *fèves à la crème* (broad beans with cream) from Elizabeth David's 1955 *Summer Cooking*. The second is for lima beans in cream from Edna Lewis's 1976 *The Taste of Country Cooking*. The third is *aubergines à la crème* from Roy Andries de Groot's resplendent 1973 *The Auberge of the Flowering Hearth*.

All three struck me as daring for their simplicity and old-world, country treatment of vegetables and cream. But in years of fantasizing, I could not bring myself to follow any. The three recipes must have found themselves in close vicinity in the recesses of my mind one summer day, when it occurred to me that they would be best combined. Here they are, in an elegant and gratifying summer gratin.

LIMAS AND EGGPLANTS À LA CRÈME

1 pound lima beans in the pod
large bouquet garni of fresh rosemary, fresh thyme, a bay leaf, a
    stalk of celery, and a fennel stalk, if you have one
2 cloves garlic, unpeeled (if you can get fresh summer garlic, do,
    and use 3 cloves)
kosher salt
good olive oil
5 Asian eggplants
2 tablespoons fresh coriander seeds, or 1 tablespoon dried
2 to 3 tablespoons heavy cream

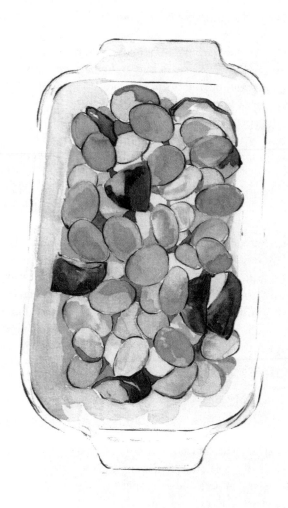

Heat the oven to 400 degrees. Shuck the lima beans and put them in a small pot with water just to cover, the bouquet garni, 1 garlic clove, and a hefty pinch of salt. Bring to a boil. Lower the heat to just below a simmer, skim any foam, and add a few pours of olive oil. Cook until all the beans are completely tender and absolutely delicious, adjusting the salt as you taste. Let the beans cool in their liquid, then drain, reserving the cooking liquid.

Cut the eggplants into oblique pieces—cut at an angle, roll the eggplant 90 degrees, and cut on the same angle again—and toss with a lot of olive oil and salt. Roast in a single layer on a baking sheet until completely tender.

Pound the remaining garlic clove and the coriander seeds to a paste with a tiny pinch of salt. Cover with olive oil to make a just-oily paste. Mix the hot roasted eggplant with the garlic-coriander oil. (The lima beans and eggplants can be cooked in advance and the results left to cool, then brought back to room temperature before proceeding.)

Set the oven to broil. Remove the garlic and bouquet garni from the beans. In a shallow gratin or roasting pan, combine the eggplant and lima beans and add enough lima bean cooking liquid to keep things moist. Make sure some of the darkened edges of the eggplant are peeking out of the top of the gratin. Pour the cream over and broil for 5 or so minutes, until bubbling and browned on top.

The effect is subtle and soothing as a river.

But what is my pompous invention but a smoothed-out succotash? Succotash, which demands more tracing than I have time to do, emerged naturally from Algonquin agriculture of beans and corn, and has remained largely unchanged.

The most honest succotash recipes are probably unwritten and go something like: *Cook beans with whatever wild herbs appear, add corn, and serve.*

Well, here is mine:

FRESH BEAN SUCCOTASH

3 cups cooked fresh shelling beans (lima, cranberry, black-eyed
    pea, flageolet . . .)

2 tablespoons duck fat or butter
1 cup finely chopped fennel
½ cup finely chopped red onion
½ cup finely chopped celery
kosher salt
kernels from 3 ears fresh corn
¼ cup crème fraîche

Cook the shelling beans according to the directions for lima beans on page 115, reserving the cooking liquid after draining the beans. Melt the duck fat in a wide heavy sauté pan, then cook the fennel, red onion, and celery in it until completely tender, salting them as they cook. Add the cooked beans and a few long pours of the bean cooking liquid. When warm and bubbling, add the corn and cook for 2 to 3 minutes, until just cooked through. Add the crème fraîche and serve warm or at room temperature.

This may be given some polish by the addition of a splash of red wine vinegar at the end, or some fresh herbs, or bits of fried bacon, or fried shallots, which will make it seem done up.

Both lima beans and eggplants *à la crème* and succotash can be treated as a main dish, served with *riz au fromage* (page 132) or some herbed or buttered rice. Both are also truly fine with battered and crisply fried fish.

"Italian spinach is as much better than French spinach as French spinach is than American spinach," wrote Waverley Root in *The Food of Italy* in 1971. He noted elsewhere that it might be as much a matter of seed as technique. Jane Grigson averred, with admirable lack of national bias, that "the thought of spinach is a pleasure." The best spinach I've ever had was Italian in seed and technique. It was moreover and unexpectedly creamed. To describe my mind I must mix the observations of the other two: the thought of Italian creamed spinach is a pleasure with few equals. This is the recipe I was given in broken English and well-formed gesture for a dish I ate in Italy one shadowy day long ago.

ITALIAN CREAMED SPINACH

3 pounds spinach, washed
3 tablespoons olive oil, plus more if needed
6 to 8 tablespoons (¾ to 1 stick) unsalted butter
kosher salt
1½ cups freshly grated Parmesan cheese

Wash the spinach. Cook it in two or three batches until just wilted in a large pan over high heat, with just the water clinging to its leaves from washing, adding the barest drizzle of olive oil if needed to keep from sticking. Drain in a colander, pushing to rid it of all liquid—which can be saved for vegetable soups—then wrap in a clean dish towel and drain completely, wringing the dish towel like a wet washcloth, until it is completely dry. Purée in a food processor or chop very finely by hand.

In the same pan, melt the butter in the olive oil over medium heat. Add the spinach and salt to taste and cook, letting it fry slowly, 2 to 4 minutes. Once it tastes good, turn off the heat and add the Parmesan, mixing well. Serve immediately or reheat in a little butter or olive oil before serving.

It seems a hideous amount of butter. In fact, it *is:* eight tablespoons for three pounds of spinach, cooked down to an insufficient several servings. The measurements are, alas, right. It is the mad case with spinach and butter—as with potatoes and butter, as with egg yolks and olive oil—that the more the first *can* absorb of the second, the closer you get to fine. The best potato purées will be impregnated with butter; the best mayonnaise contains every drop of olive oil it can, and tastes not of egg or oil but of ambrosia.

According to Jane Grigson, *her* best spinach is a French recipe, in which "spinach was cooked and reheated over five days. Each day butter was added, so that by the end half a kilo [2.2 pounds] had absorbed about 300 grams [2½ sticks] of butter."

FOUR-DAY SPINACH

Note: This recipe of unusual deliciousness shows the ability of spinach to absorb butter. I believe one can go on adding butter to it for seven days, but at the end of four days it looks and tastes so good that it has to be eaten.

3 to 4 pounds spinach, washed
1 pound unsalted butter
kosher salt, freshly ground black pepper, freshly grated nutmeg,
    lemon juice

Day 1: *Cook the spinach and drain it in the usual way. Chop it roughly before adding 4 ounces of butter; keep the pan over a good heat until the butter is absorbed. Leave to cool in a clean pudding basin. Store in the refrigerator.*

    Day 2: *Reheat the spinach with another 4 ounces of butter. Leave to cool.*

    Days 3 and 4: *Repeat day two, except that on the fourth day the spinach will be served hot and not be left to cool.*

    You will have a rich, dark green purée, a cream or sauce rather than a vegetable. Spinach for adults, decidedly.

When should one add the salt, pepper, nutmeg, lemon juice? I'm unqualified to answer. Out of implacable impatience, I've never made it past day two. But on my own, I add salt tentatively, a little each day, leaving buffer to adjust. I grate in nutmeg and sprinkle lemon juice when I surrender to temptation, just before eating.

Nor am I credible on what to serve *with* four-day spinach. I can offer only that if I spent four days, four pounds of spinach, and a pound of butter on a dish, the rest of the meal would be lightly chilled red wine and toast. (Or rice.)

Both Jane Grigson and her compatriot Elizabeth David have enticing recipes for green bean and almond soup. Both include garlic, left out of the aloof nineteenth-century classic green beans amandine. By their wisdoms, I've added it, and a great deal of lemon and herbs. This is especially good when beans are young and thin.

GARLICKY GREEN BEANS AMANDINE

about 2 pounds very thin green beans
kosher salt
olive oil
3 cloves green garlic or 1 clove cured garlic
½ cup chopped mixed fresh herbs (fennel fronds, parsley,
    marjoram, celery leaf)
zest and juice of ½ lemon
¼ teaspoon pounded coriander seeds, ideally fresh
½ cup almonds, toasted and roughly chopped

Bring a large pot of water to a boil. Trim the stem end of the beans. Salt the water to taste like pleasant seawater. Boil the beans in batches, removing them to a waiting tray the instant they are cooked through. Drizzle lightly with olive oil as you remove them. Reserve ¼ cup of the water.

Pound the garlic into a paste with a big pinch of salt. Once it has become a paste, transfer it to a mortar or food processor, add the herbs, and pound into the paste, then add the lemon zest, coriander, and enough olive oil to move things around. Add the almonds and pulse (or pound) to chop until broken down into large, irregular pieces. Tip into a bowl and add enough olive oil to easily mix with a spoon with some oil pooling. Add the beans, half the reserved cooking water, and the lemon juice. Mix well, adding more water if needed to keep it from becoming too dry. Taste and adjust the salt.

These are wonderful with pork chops. Any that are leftover can be combined with fresh ricotta for a summery open-faced sandwich or small crisp appetizer toasts.

For years I have cooked *petits pois à la française*, a classic French preparation of green peas and lettuce, under the impression that I was following a classic recipe I'd read in *How to Cook a Wolf.*

I intended to pass along an old wisdom, unchanged. But I find myself rebuked, having been tricked by my own memory—like most of its species in a constant state of half-eclipse. My *petits pois à la française*, which I think an ideal combination of sweet butter, wilted lettuce, fresh peas, and bacon lardons, is not M.F.K. Fisher's—hers has no lardons, which to me are such a part of the experience—nor my next guess, Elizabeth David's, nor even Ali-Bab's, whose entry on the dish in *Gastronomie Pratique* was my last best stab at my source. Ali-Bab's doesn't even contain lettuce . . . After wondering if I'd dreamed my version up entirely, I was informed not overly gently that this is my brother's recipe, almost exactly. It seems he taught it to me, and I learned, then forgot the teacher but kept the wisdom.

PETITS POIS À LA FRANÇAISE

½ cup bacon lardons, in batons or little cubes
4 tablespoons (½ stick) unsalted butter
1 cup diced or sliced spring onion
kosher salt
water or broth, as needed
4 cups fresh shelled peas or just-thawed frozen peas
2 cups romaine lettuce cut into ribbons
optional: freshly ground black pepper

Render the lardons over low heat for 3 to 5 minutes. Add the butter. Once it melts, add the spring onion. Sprinkle lightly with salt. Cook, stirring frequently, for 5 to 10 minutes, adding water to keep the onion from browning—there can be a bit of liquid left in the pan. Once the onion is completely tender, add the peas. Stir through, and cook, keeping it brothy and adding liquid if needed, until the peas are just cooked. Add the romaine, stir through, then turn off the heat. Taste for salt and adjust, still in the pan. Add black pepper, if you like.

The whole production takes less than fifteen minutes and leaves the same impression Thai dishes do—of having demanded a kind of finicky focus and skill, even when they are fast and basic. It is the effect of the balance of elements in a dish, which, like the balance of elements in a conversation or fellow human, can leave one feeling calm.

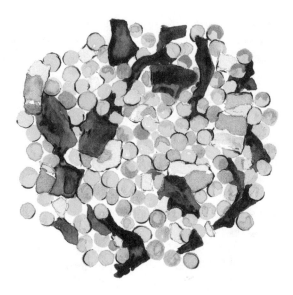

In my dream scenario, each diner would get a deep white porcelain bowlful, with an extra-large spoon, and eat only sweet peas, bacon, and buttery lettuce until he or she could sit back, satisfied and already dreaming. Of course there could be bread . . .

That many peas take hours to shell, so unless it is only two of you, I recommend, my head firmly returned from the clouds, also serving a roast chicken, or fish cooked quickly in butter with a splash of wine and herbs added once it is out of the pan. Or a whole roast fish, with herbs tied in its middle and good olive oil to be passed at the table. For such a realistic meal, as Aldo Buzzi would say, "And the wine, let it be cool!"

There is no definitive answer to the question of why the children of one era are depressed by the turnip while the children of another are invigorated by it. It only adds to the mystery that in every age there is a fruit that used to be vegetable, a vegetable that used to be weed, a weed that used to be medicine, and an ingredient served only raw and fresh as dawn that used to be cooked as though it were a dried bean. (And some animal bit considered firmly inedible that was lately a gourmand's highest delicacy.)

Tomatoes are today salad vegetables, to slice and arrange on sun-warmed plates. They are still cooked, but only into sauce or soup. Until fifty years ago, however, they were broiled and stewed and fried as readily as green Italian squash. Here is a recipe for broiled tomatoes for those who will not be prisoners to their age.

HERBED TOMATOES

6 medium summer tomatoes
¼ cup olive oil, plus more for drizzling
kosher salt
2 tablespoons chopped green garlic or 1 tablespoon chopped
    cured garlic
¼ cup finely chopped fresh cilantro, stems included
2 tablespoons finely chopped fresh Thai basil leaves

Cut the tomatoes across their equators. Scoop out some of their seeds and juice without completely disemboweling them. Heat a large cast-iron pan or grill. Lightly drizzle the pan with olive oil. Cook the tomatoes in a single layer, cut sides down, for 3 to 4 minutes, until they just start to collapse when plucked at and the cut sides are browned. Turn off the heat. Turn the tomatoes over and cook for 3 minutes on the second side. Remove to a plate, cut sides up, and lightly salt.

In a mortar or on a cutting board, pound the garlic to a paste with a pinch of salt. Stir in the chopped herbs and olive oil. Taste for salt and adjust.

Divide the herb paste among the cut sides of the tomatoes, using it all, making a thick, herby blanket on each. Eat warm or at room temperature or cool.

This is almost endlessly variable. Use parsley instead of cilantro and basil, and add an anchovy fillet or two. Add crisp fried breadcrumbs or fried shallots, either to the mix or sprinkled over top. And why not add citrus zest to the herb paste? Or olives, or capers, or bits of pecorino cheese, and, once they are out of the pan, fresh fava beans . . .

Whatever else you find lying about can be your further guide. Half the fun is imprecision, for any amount of anything that tastes good itself can be added with immunity. If you are inclined, forget the recipe and keep the wisdom that tomatoes, topped with fragrant whatnots, are delicious broiled.

Equally delicious are buttered tomatoes on toast.

BUTTERED TOMATOES ON TOAST

4½ to 5 tablespoons unsalted butter
½ large white onion, chopped (about 1⅓ cups)
½ to 1 teaspoon kosher salt
2 cloves garlic, chopped
3 sprigs thyme
1 bay leaf
10 to 12 canned whole peeled tomatoes and a little of the juice
4 slices brown bread, toasted at the last moment

Melt 2½ to 3 tablespoons of the butter in a medium pot. The instant it stops sizzling, add the onion and salt. Cook until the onion is tender,

10 to 12 minutes, adding the garlic, thyme, and bay leaf 5 minutes in. Add the tomatoes, smashing them with a wooden spoon. Cook, stirring occasionally, for 20 minutes, adding a little tomato juice from the can or water if the mixture begins to brown.

Butter the toast with ½ tablespoon of the remaining butter per piece, "wall to wall." Spread the tomatoes thickly over the crisp brown toast and eat immediately.

These make a comforting lunch with sliced avocado or boiled eggs. Or with green beans, perhaps turned amandine, and creamed spinach, they are dinner.

Cucumbers are another once-cooked vegetable now relegated to the salad plate. Here they are cooked again. These are fast and truly delicious atop a bowl of hot rice.

SWEET-AND-SPICY CUCUMBERS

1½ large cucumbers, peeled
1 tablespoon olive oil
2 cloves garlic, sliced
½ teaspoon kosher salt
2 dried chiles, crumbled
⅛ teaspoon sugar
1 teaspoon chopped fresh mint, basil, cilantro, or scallion greens

Halve the cucumbers lengthwise and scoop out the seeds. Cut them into ⅓-inch-thick half-moons. Heat the olive oil in a cast-iron pan or wok. Add the garlic and half the salt. When the garlic is just softened, add the chiles and spread it all out to sizzle. The instant the garlic has begun to turn golden, add the cucumbers in a single layer along with the remaining salt; cook, stirring only occasionally, letting the garlic and chiles darken if they do. When the cucumbers have begun to get nicely cooked, add the sugar and stir through. Cook until the cucumbers are just tender and beginning to seem translucent, 5 to 6 minutes total. Turn off the heat, add the herbs, and serve.

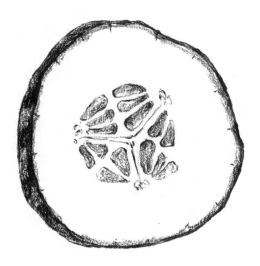

There are too many tempting vegetable recipes from earlier times for me to include. I wish for a whole book, rather than a few slim pages, to dedicate to little onions in cream, gratinéed endives with ham, mushrooms with crème fraîche and herbs . . .

But on second thought, those, and hundreds more that fit the old formula might simply have a *new* formula applied. Yes, it might be: *Vegetable, cooked in salted water and oil until tender when pierced with a sharp knife, lightly basted with good fresh cream* [if you like it], *broiled until just brown, then showered with fresh herbs.* In other words, treated with less finicky finesse than they were for the 150 years before ours, and less daintiness demanded of them.

But I am only suggesting that vegetables be treated as they were earlier yet, in less prosperous times, before Escoffier, before Fannie Farmer even, when there was *less* water, *less* butter, *less* cream. On final consideration, in the words of H. A. Rey, "It may be even that the new way is not so new after all."

AN AUTUMN LUNCH

Crudités of radishes and fennel
with lime sauce

Clam bouillon

Riz au fromage

Limas and eggplants à la crème

Wine: A creamy but zesty, salty white
Example: Chablis
Christian Moreau Chablis 2015

Chocolate mousse

TO RISE LIKE RICE

Starches and Eggs

V

Thay Boile it as we Due Rise and Eat it
with Bairs greas and Sugar.

—A fur trader

W hat gave our hapless trader the impression of being cooked as
we do "rise"? I imagine it was wild rice, on the wet wild plains
of Montana, which is not rice at all but a species of aquatic grass.

We eat less wild rice than we used to—fashion has turned toward
Asian rice preparations, and all over Asia the stalk of the wild *Zizania*
grass is cooked as a vegetable and the seed left behind to continue the
bloodline. The last fifty years have, however, smiled on the cookery
of tame rice. After centuries of insult verging on torment, it is no
longer overcooked. We understand (better . . .) how it is eaten where
it is sacramental bread. Today, rice is springy. Things are simpler and
they are better.

There are nonetheless several old-fashioned rice recipes that
become very good dishes as long as their rice is not cooked to a soft
pulp and they're kept from brimming over with cream and cheese—
in other words, as long as the seeds' own intrinsic limits are respected.

The best example is *riz au fromage*. There are many variations, most
dealing reasonably, if heavy-handedly, with their two main ingredients: rice and cheese. *Riz au fromage* is (obviously) a French dish,
often made, in its homeland, with *fromage blanc*. In twentieth-century
America, it was rice and cheese (too often, if innocently) made with
quick-cooking Minute rice and cheddar. In Italy, it is called *torta di
riso* (rice tart), made simply in the Italian coastal city of Genova with

a fresh cheese called *prescinsêua* and pearly Italian short-grained rice.
I make *riz au fromage* as that Italian rice tart.

RIZ AU FROMAGE

2 cups Arborio, Carnaroli, or Vialone Nano rice
2 cups whole milk
2 cups water
kosher salt
2 tablespoons olive oil, plus more as needed
2 eggs, beaten
2 heaping tablespoons freshly grated Parmesan cheese
just over 8 ounces fresh ricotta cheese

*Heat the oven to 355 degrees. Rinse and drain the rice. Combine the
milk and water in a medium pot and bring to a boil. Once it's boiling,
add a pinch of salt—it should be less salty than pasta water. Add the
rice and cook over low heat until al dente. Turn off the heat and leave
to cool. When no longer warm to the touch, add the olive oil. Wait
ten minutes, then add the eggs, Parmesan, and half the ricotta. Heat
a large heavy oven-safe pan over high heat, then coat the bottom with
olive oil. Press the rice mixture into the pan in a thin layer. Turn off
the heat, add the remaining ricotta in spoonfuls over the rice, pressing
it in, and bake for about 10 minutes, until set. Switch the oven to broil
and quickly brown the top. Serve hot or at room temperature, cut into
slices.*

The intent men and women who watch over *torta di riso* batter in
Genova's narrow galleys called *sciamadde* cook it in battered shallow
steel pans directly over coals. They simultaneously cook the golden
chickpea pancake called *farinata* and dip tiny shrimp, curls of squid,
and whitebait the thickness of a goose quill into hot oil to fry. These
quick-minded souls cut their tarts with old shears and serve pieces
on cardboard for eating immediately or taking home. Any big frying
pan, or, even better, a *paella* pan, works, as long as it is gotten quite

hot, especially when one keeps in mind how it looks in Genova—rustic and uneven and probably as unlike real *riz au fromage* as a dish of rice and cheese could be.

This is as suitable as risotto as a main dish, and also a faultless picnic food, good for wrapping in wax paper and eating cool.

Riz à la Georgienne is buttered rice. The combination is timeless, and its ingredient list shows admirable brevity, at least François Tanty's in his 1893 *La Cuisine Française: French Cooking for Every Home, Adapted to American Requirements*. It reads: *Rice . . . 1 lb Butter . . . ¼ pound Time . . . ½ hour*. (This is the only book I have in which Time is listed as an ingredient, as I am reminded it should be each time I see it.)

My favorite *riz à la Georgienne* recipe comes from *Good Things to Eat*, from 1911, by the irreproachable Rufus Estes, a freed slave who became a Pullman car steward, then a chef. Mr. Estes's single literary effort is probably my favorite cookbook. His recipes are beautiful and clear. He writes with a mannerly diction that barely suppresses his voluptuary heart. I share his tastes.

When I turned to compare Mr. Estes's and M. Tanty's recipes and my own general system, I discovered that Mr. Estes, whom I've long silently considered a friend, had plagiarized Tanty's rice-cooking technique, word for word.

It is a mean skulduggery . . . and natural. I, like him, can't think of a more vivid description of draining rice after boiling than M. Tanty's:

> Wash one pound of rice in several changes of cold water until water is clear, and cook until soft, but not soft enough to mash between the fingers. Let it drip, cool and drip again.

Rufus (for surely we are on a first name basis by now) adds an essential detail: not to brown the butter when melting, which makes the rice too rich and nutty; he also alters the cooking time from fifteen minutes in the oven to twenty, which depends on your rice and your oven but is right for mine. Each time I make this finely named buttered rice I feel in the company of Rufus, whom I consider even more my friend now that I'm acquainted with one of his foibles.

RIZ À LA GEORGIENNE

1 pound jasmine rice
kosher salt
5 tablespoons butter
1 bay leaf
1 cup chopped fresh parsley or a combination parsley and dill

Heat the oven to 375 degrees. Bring a large pot of water to a boil. Put the rice in a colander and rinse it briefly. Once the water boils, salt it well, like pasta water. Cook the rice like pasta, removing it with a sieve or draining it through a fine-mesh sieve when it's just cooked—making sure to watch it drip (once will suffice) before emptying it onto a baking sheet to cool. Melt the butter. Combine the butter, rice, and bay leaf in an oven-safe pot with a lid and cook in the oven, covered, for 15 minutes, or until the butter has melted and been absorbed and the rice is tender. Mix the herbs through and serve.

This is delicious with chicken in leftover wine (page 164), or not-chicken fricassee (page 162), or roasted vegetables, or soft-cooked eggs. Or a ladleful of stewed beans or lentils, perhaps with sausages, or frankfurters (why not?) cut into coins and simmered in the beans' warmth. Or beneath an omelet or scrambled eggs with herbs.

If buttered rice is too buttery for you, then pilaf is the dish.

There are wonderful Russian and Uzbek and Ukrainian pilafs, called *plovs*, of beef or chicken, spiced rice, and rich broth, finished with a tangle of chicken fat–fried onions and a dollop of sour cream for gloss. There are then again Indian *pilaus* of fish, peas, spiced vegetables, and coconut oil or ghee, with yogurt sauces and chutneys for dabbing. Then there are the pilafs served in America when my mother was a child, which as an adult she cooked for her children: white rice, sautéed with onion, then simmered in broth, perhaps scattered with sliced almonds, an elegant alternative to plain white rice. The American pilaf is a skimpy variation on a festive dish. But it has a restrained appeal, drawn from the flourishes of butter, herbs (which

I add, if I have them, by unrestrained handfuls at the end), and broth that distinguish it from the good-but-plain rice one makes in a hurry on a Monday night. This, with a buttery roast chicken, is a consummate happy dinner.

MY MOTHER'S RICE PILAF

½ cup chopped white onion
2 tablespoons butter
2 cups long-grain white rice
3 cups rich chicken broth, with its fat, if homemade
1 dried chile
bouquet garni of 1 sprig thyme, parsley stems, and a bay leaf
optional: a big handful of chopped fresh parsley, cilantro, or dill,
    or all combined

Heat the oven to 400 degrees. Sauté the onion in the butter in an oven-safe pot or casserole until you can break it with a spoon. Add the rice and cook for a few more minutes. Add the broth and chile. Bring to a boil. Place the bouquet garni on top. Cover, transfer to the oven, and bake for 17 minutes. Remove the chile and mix the herbs through just before serving, if using.

A fine addition to a basic pilaf is any of a roast chicken's attendant juices, which can make up part of the volume of broth, if the chicken has already been roasted, and will only add to the rice's savourousness.

Croquettes of all varieties once populated French and American meal schemes like dandelions on spring lawns. There are hundreds of theories about their origin. Croquettes of béchamel sauce may have been born in an Enlightenment-era kitchen oubliette; rice croquettes may be Moorish or Chinese or Indian . . . Did potato-based croquettes originate in North and South America because the potato did?

I don't know. A definition of croquettes from the *Dictionnaire de l'académie des Gastronomes* (Paris, 1962) reads: "A fried and elongated dumpling. Etymology: derives from croquer, 'to crunch.' Gastronomy:

The croquette is rolled in flour, breadcrumbs, fine breadcrumbs, and deep fried." The *Dictionnaire* says nothing of whither the croquette itself, or whether the croquette is to be potato or béchamel or rice. Croquettes of rice—the starchy, short-grained Italian kind—are the simplest to make, a good way of using what is left from other dishes, and delightful to crunch.

CRISP RICE CROQUETTES

Note: This makes 10 to 12 croquettes. I can think of no reason not to double or triple the recipe and freeze some, un-breaded, to fry another day.

2 to 3 cups chicken broth or water
3 tablespoons butter
½ white onion, finely chopped
kosher salt
1 cup Arborio, Carnaroli, or Vialone Nano rice
¼ cup white wine
1 cup grated Parmesan cheese
½ to ⅔ cup leftover meat or stew, like those on pages 185–192
2 tablespoons chopped fresh mozzarella cheese
all-purpose flour
2 eggs, beaten
white breadcrumbs
grapeseed, canola, or olive oil
flaky salt, for serving
1 lemon, wedged, for serving

Make the simplest risotto: Bring the broth to a simmer. Melt the butter in a pot, add the onion, season with salt, and cook until it is tender but not browned. Add the rice and stir until the grains are buttered and opaque. Add the wine and cook to just dry. Add the simmering broth ladle by ladle, stirring regularly and waiting for each to be absorbed before adding the next, until the rice is tender, 20 to 25 minutes. (It may only take 2 cups of the liquid.) Remove from the heat, add the Parmesan, taste, and adjust the salt. It should be highly seasoned. Cool.

Make the croquettes: Scoop a portion of the cooled rice into your palm and spread it into a pancake. Fill the center with ¼ teaspoon of meat and a few cubes of mozzarella—if you use leftover poached chicken or fish, add a drizzle of olive oil and cream to it and mix before using as a filling. Close each pancake into a ball—or to be à l'Academie, a torpedo shape—around the filling, enclosing it completely.

Put the flour in a shallow dish and season it lightly with salt. Put the egg in a second dish and the breadcrumbs in a third. Roll each croquette in the flour, then dip in the beaten egg, and then roll in the breadcrumbs. Heat 1 inch of grapeseed oil in a heavy pot. Fry in batches in the hot oil. Drain briefly on a kitchen towel. Serve very hot, topped with flaky salt with lemon wedges on the side.

These croquettes and a crisp salad are as fine a meal as the meat or stew to which they are heir. The mixture ripens well and can be made into croquettes for several days.

What is true of progress in rice cookery is also true of noodles—today widely called "pasta." There is no question *pastasciutta* (dried pasta) and fresh egg pappardelle and linguine and tagliatelle are made and treated more intelligently today than a century ago, when cooks followed Mrs. Beeton's rule of leaving "1½ to 1¾ hour to boil the macaroni." And gummed the result briefly before spitting it out, one is tempted to fastidiously add.

Here are two pasta recipes from earlier days that deserve to be treated with the Italian terseness that we now recognize as the Right Way.

With the five ingredients listed in Richard Olney's 1970 *The French Menu Cookbook*—"1 pound short macaroni; salted boiling water, cooking liquid from daube [stew]; freshly grated nutmeg; freshly grated Parmesan"—a classic *macaronade* rivals *riz à la Georgienne* for pithiness. It is moreover a frugal scheme, as a *macaronade* is an afterthought of any stew. Its making should follow the theory of Patricia Wells, who writes in her *Bistro Cooking*: "To prepare an authentic *macaronade*, you must first prepare a meat stew, either an *estouffade* or a daube . . ." It is a wise, unquestioning plan. You must make a stew, and even eat some of it, to get to what lies on its other side. *Macaronade* is the rare dish from far-gone days to which I've added ingredients, finding the original spare, even to my sometimes Spartan tastes.

MACARONADE

2 tablespoons unsalted butter, plus more for buttering the
     baking dish
kosher salt
1 pound dried rigatoni
2 cups sauciest cooking liquid from meat stew, meat included
     (see recipe for daube Provençal, page 189)
½ cup grated Parmesan cheese
½ cup fresh ricotta cheese

Butter a large baking dish. Bring a large pot of water to a boil. Salt it a little lightly for pasta. Cook the pasta in the boiling water until al dente.

Remove the cooked pasta to a waiting bowl. Mix with the butter. Add the stew and cooking liquid. Mix and let sit for 15 minutes. Add half the pasta to the baking dish. Top with half the Parmesan, then the remaining pasta, then the remaining Parmesan. Top with dollops of ricotta. Let sit for 15 minutes, or cover and refrigerate for up to 2 nights before baking. Bring to room temperature before baking. Set the broiler to high. Bake the macaronade *under the broiler until the top is slightly crisped and the ricotta has begun to brown.*

This is a hearty but subtle baked dish, with faint glimmers of sweet spice and overall smooth wholesomeness, especially if you have used daube Provençal. It is also variable. Why use rigatoni if you have large shell-shaped pasta, and moreover children who will delight in being served three shells each, all to themselves? Why limit yourself to daube Provençal when the refrigerator holds the last of your *blanquette* or, more probably, honest chicken and mushroom casserole? If your stew or casserole is a thin soup, better to be patient and listen to Patricia Wells and first make a stew or daube or *estouffade* than try to get directly to *macaronade*. There is, as far as I can tell, no way around the stew but through it.

A great number of the *"à la"* dishes of classic cuisine make sense, and provide the amateur culinary anthropologist what is called, too cannily, food for thought. *À l'alsacienne* means made with sauerkraut, as almost anything in Alsace was and—fortunately for those of us who love it—still is. *À la Périgueux* indicates truffles— of which the best come from Perigord. *À la vigneronne* means cooked in grape leaves (among other things; winemakers eat well). *À la chartreuse* includes an array of vegetables, after the vegetarian Chartreux monks. *À la diable* is deviled; *à la flamande* has cabbage, carrots, and turnips; *à l'italienne* noodles; *à la Lucullus* truffles, foie gras, and Madeira (!).

This edifying list continues for a mile, delivering eloquent lessons on Latin roots and cultural habits, but for one or two notable exceptions. The most intriguing to me has always been *à la Godard*. Beside it one finds, upon investigation, in *Explanations of All Terms Used in Coockery* (sic), the tautological: "with Godard garniture." This, according to Charles Herman Senn's 1862 *The Menu Book*, includes: "Slices of sweetbread, small chicken quenelles, cocks' combs, mushroom heads, and sliced truffle, madera sauce or demi-glace." Höfler lists quenelles, lamb or veal sweetbreads, truffles, and mushrooms, with a 1691 citation that's still more complex. In *The Epicurean*, Charles Ranhofer gives a recipe for "Tenderloin of Beef à la Godard," which ends: "set the tenderloin on top and garnish around with twelve truffles cooked in Madeira wine, twelve fine mushrooms heads grooved and turned round, and twelve cocks' combs. Moisten with a little half-glaze. Set around twelve oval quenelles decorated with red beef tongue . . ."

From my point of view, the Godard garnishes seem likely to produce such strong physical effects on the tongue and libido that they should be handled more sparingly or else just be defined as an orgy.

My own prudish culinary imagination has shaped *à la Godard* sauce into a *ragù*. Here is a recipe concocted, like so many I've stewarded from past to present, by my brother. It contains the light pleasant tang of offal and mustiness of mushroom, and is so velvety it adheres to the noodles as though born as their skin. Its ingredients and method are common.

MACARONI À LA À LA GODARD

½ cup olive oil, plus more as needed
1 pound fresh chicken livers
kosher salt
¾ cup red wine
1½ cups dried porcini mushrooms, rehydrated in at least 2 cups
    boiling water
3 tablespoons butter
½ pound ground beef
1 cup finely diced onion
½ cup finely diced carrot
½ cup finely diced celery
4 cloves garlic, finely chopped
2 teaspoons chopped fresh rosemary
1 tablespoon chopped fresh sage

½ cup chopped fresh parsley
½ teaspoon whole fennel seeds
1 teaspoon tomato paste
2 tablespoons cognac
1 cup heavy cream
2 teaspoons red wine vinegar
1 pound pasta in a shape with edges, like orecchiette or
    quadrefiore
Parmesan cheese, for grating

Heat a large pan over high heat. Add a small amount of olive oil and sear the livers very briefly on each side in one or two batches, seasoning with salt as you remove them from the pan. Deglaze the pan with a little bit of the red wine between batches or with ½ cup of the wine at the end. Pour the deglazing liquid over the livers.

Drain the mushrooms through a fine colander set over a bowl, reserving the liquid, and finely chop.

Melt 1 tablespoon butter in a little olive oil. Add the beef. Cook, breaking up the meat, until beginning to brown. Add the mushrooms. Cook together until well browned, seasoning with salt when almost done. Remove the meat and mushrooms. Deglaze the pan with the remaining wine. Pour the deglazing liquid over the browned meat and mushrooms.

Heat the pan again over high heat. Add the remaining olive oil. Cook the onion, carrot, and celery over medium heat until they are completely soft and have begun to caramelize, adding the garlic near the end. Add the herbs and fennel seeds. Cook until fragrant, then add the tomato paste and cook until it, too, caramelizes. Deglaze the pan with the cognac, stirring, and cook until the pan is almost completely dry. Add the beef and mushrooms and 1½ cups of the mushroom soaking liquid. Cook over low heat, at a bare simmer, until reduced by three-quarters.

Dice the livers and tip them into the pan, along with the demiglace and the cream. Cook over low heat, partially covered, until the livers are cooked through. Remove from the heat and add the vinegar.

Bring a large pot of water to a boil. Salt it well so it tastes like seawater. Cook the pasta in the boiling water until nearly done. Remove some of the ragù from the pan. Add the pasta to the pan along with 2 tablespoons butter, and mix well, grating Parmesan over the top generously as you mix. Add more ragù *if you like, or save for* ragù-*topped toasts. Serve with more grated Parmesan cheese on top.*

Both *macaronade* and pasta *à la à la Godard* have such fine sauces that they are especially good fodder for that rustic Italian habit of turning leftover pasta into frittatas. For this, there is a single formula: Mix 2 or 3 cups cold, sauced pasta with 3 beaten eggs, salt it lightly, add any parsley you have, chopped, and, if you have it, Parmesan cheese, grated directly into the mixture, and cook it, starting on the stove and continuing it in the oven at 375 degrees for 10 to 15 minutes, until the top is firm to the touch. Invert onto a plate and serve your *frittata à la macaroni à la à la Godard* with a great flourish, and speaking its name with the dramatic trills of *La Traviata.*

Perhaps the simplest of somewhat forgotten starch dishes is crêpes. These forgiving concoctions of egg, melted butter, milk, and flour, a staple of last century, are elegant—imagine a pancake at a tenth its thickness—and both literally and figuratively pliable, a helpful mix-and-match sort of dish to have up one's sleeve, as ready to be filled with leftover coq au vin or buttered zucchini or butter and jam. I do not know why crêpes disappeared from our menus, other than that French dishes fell out of vogue. But if you can bring yourself to measure out flour, eggs, and milk, you will find yourself with a dish that is simpler than pancakes and more adaptable. Here is a recipe, which includes roasted wild mushrooms, one of its most satisfying appurtenances.

HERBED CRÊPES WITH MUSHROOMS

1½ cups all-purpose flour
3 large eggs, beaten
2½ cups whole milk
3 tablespoons butter, melted
a heaping ¼ teaspoon kosher salt, plus to taste
up to 1 cup mixed fresh herbs (parsley, dill, fennel fronds,
    tarragon, etc.)
1 pound mixed wild mushrooms
olive oil
1 sprig rosemary
1 clove garlic, lightly smashed
optional: crème fraîche or unsweetened whipped cream

Add the flour to the beaten eggs, then add the milk, then the melted butter. Whisk well. (I whisk well, but I'm told that in France, crêpes are stirred with a spoon so as not to incorporate air. I don't know who's right. What is good for the goose might not be good for the gander. Choose sides and hope for the best.) Add salt and herbs and let rest at room temperature 2 to 3 hours.

Heat the oven to 400 degrees. Stem and halve or roughly slice the mushrooms. Toss with olive oil and roast on a baking pan with the sprig of rosemary and the garlic until just beginning to crisp, 10 to 15 minutes. Remove from the oven and season with salt.

Heat a lightly oiled crêpe pan or other small cured frying pan over medium heat. Add just enough batter to thinly coat the bottom of the pan—the amount varies depending on your pan size; you may want to experiment with the first few. Cook until the surface bubbles and the edges just begin to brown, about 30 seconds, then turn the crêpe over with your fingers—it is not at all delicate, though it seems like it would be—and cook for 10 seconds or so more. The first crêpes are always ugly, and can be given as a treat to a friend or child or pet. Continue, occasionally re-oiling the pan between crêpes. They will shortly improve and you'll feel like a cognoscente. Stack the crêpes, as you finish them, on a plate covered with a dish towel until you're ready to eat.

Serve with the roasted mushrooms and a bowl of crème fraîche, if you want.

These have a lovely proven habit of seeming different each time their fillings change. Boiled or scrambled eggs, with a scattering of parsley or chives, are a wonderful variation. Several cured white anchovies are also delicious in the arrangement. There is little that isn't, whether cooked broccoli rabe; or poached chicken pulled to aromatic bits, mixed with herbs, lemon juice, and ricotta; or leftover mashed potatoes, quickly hashed with freshly fried onion and garam masala and cilantro; or roasted squash, smashed and brightened with lemon and Parmesan . . . Of course, the herbs could be removed from the batter, or substituted with scrapes of dried spice.

I have recently become guardian of a sourdough starter who demands of me that I use her every week or so, which I have been obediently doing via sourdough pancakes, as I am a bad bread maker with no talent or inclination to improve. These are just as good in the savory arrangements above. I have learned that, even if they are cool and have been sitting on a tray on the kitchen table since breakfast, leftover pancakes, which I am unwilling to discard, can be treated like crêpes, spread with crème fraîche or goat cheese and scrambled eggs or prosciutto or leftover breakfast sausage. They make a reviving midmorning or midafternoon pick-me-up. Leftover crêpes are, of course, much more socially acceptable.

If you find you like making crêpes, purchase a pound of buckwheat flour. This is no more flour than wild rice is rice. Buckwheat flour is ground seeds, and produces a nutty version of the crêpe on page 143. In Brittany, birthplace of the crêpe, these are somewhat confusingly called *galettes*—elsewhere in France the name for freeform tarts, best made probably with small hard apples, or fresh peaches, or sour cherries with a sprinkling of sugar on top . . .

The strong-flavored yet fine-bodied buckwheat pancakes are still made in Brittany, and they are delicious. Following the general idea in Roger Lallemand's 1971 *La Vraie Cuisine de la Bretagne*, to make crêpes with buckwheat, I take 1 cup buckwheat flour, add a tiny pinch of salt, and 3 eggs. With a *spoon*, according to him, or whisk, according to me, I slowly incorporate 1½ to 2 cups of water. (The amount is imprecise, and seems to depend on the buckwheat and the atmosphere.) I stop when the batter has the body of heavy cream. I let it rest at room temperature for an hour, add ¼ cup olive oil or melted butter, and proceed as on page 143.

Richard Olney recommends that crêpe batter rest in proportion to the aggression applied to its mixing. If you have whisked furiously, consider waiting longer before cooking. If your touch is feather-light, do not rest at all. If the crêpes act persnickety, some regular all-purpose flour, mixed in with moderate aggression, will mellow them out. Lallemand notes that some Bretons replace some of the water in the crêpe batter with cider. I would only do this with good Breton or maybe Basque cider, with bagpipes in the background.

It is good, economical, and vaguely dramatic to take either kind of crêpes, spread them with something rich, roll them, lay them closely side by side in a baking dish as a sort of rough crêpe casserole, and bake them until hot and bubbling. *Crêpes farcies* or *crêpes gratinées* appear more formal than the insolently casual scheme above, but are also a good way to use small amounts of herbs and cheese to make a pancake recipe into a show.

CRÊPES FARCIES

½ clove garlic, pounded to a paste with a small pinch of salt
½ cup walnuts, toasted and roughly chopped
1 tablespoon dried marjoram, or 3 tablespoons fresh
½ cup chopped fresh parsley
4 to 5 tablespoons olive oil
kosher salt
2 cups fresh ricotta cheese, or more to taste
butter
crêpes (page 143 or 145)
a good, somewhat soft but gratable melting cheese, like Gruyère
    or Comté
lemon wedges, for serving

Heat the oven to 375 degrees. In a food processor or using a mortar and pestle, combine the garlic, walnuts, marjoram, and parsley. Add the olive oil and taste, adjusting the salt. Remove half the pesto and transfer to a bowl. Add the ricotta and mix well; taste and adjust the salt again. Lightly butter a small gratin dish or roasting pan. One crêpe at a time, fill the bottom third well with the ricotta mixture, roll, and place, seam side down, in the prepared pan. Continue until all the crêpes are nestled closely in a single layer. Place on the top oven rack and bake for 12 to 15 minutes. Remove, switch the oven to broil, grate Gruyère generously over the top, and broil until the cheese has melted. Dot with the remaining pesto and serve immediately, with lemon wedges alongside.

There are countless other quick-and-easy sauces that might replace pesto. Olive paste or tapenade can be made in under five minutes by finely chopping olives, adding herbs and chopped garlic, and anchovies if you like them, and setting it all awash in good olive oil. Or it may be bought. Basil pesto is as fast if it is summer, and maintains its quiet authority as king of sauces. Most savorous pastes, as long as they taste good, work, and experimentation is encouraged.

Another way to go is to follow not the Gallic manner, but the ruddier Italian one. In Tuscany, crêpes are filled with ricotta and wild nettles. This combination tastes of the hills and wild grasses but can be simulated without too much loss with spinach, cooked and squeezed dry, then mixed with ricotta.

Then, again, the possibilities multiply. For the same can be done with kale, or the last of the roasted wild mushrooms. Or roasted asparagus, or roasted cherry tomatoes and a lot of freshly torn raw basil, or anything else, according to your preferences and needs.

If you were, in an experimental strain, to change the quantities of the basic ingredients of crêpes—butter, flour, eggs, milk, and sometimes cheese—you would find yourself with a soufflé. That seems perhaps unlikely if you have never made a soufflé. But the soufflé, like crêpes, is a dish that relies only on pantry staples and a bit of science . . . plus, the gastronomic pleasure to be found in risen foods, like yeasted breads and biscuits and soufflés, which seems to derive from the airy absence that makes their presence more sharply felt. It is a pleasure I suspect is linked to the one we feel at other risen things, like the flight of a bird or a soul released from samsara. Most of us fall, morally and physically, sometimes. Fewer of us rise, at least with the grace of fresh bread or egg whites.

To make a soufflé without being worried (which soufflé teachers from Carême or seem intent on ensuring one *is*) one must understand a bit behind why and how soufflés rise in the first place. It is a simple and digestible explanation, even to those not kitchen-chemistry inclined. A soufflé, as Harold McGee defines it in *On Food and Cooking*, is a foam. The egg at the dish's center is its engine, seeming even in this rudimentary stage skyward-bound. Egg white proteins, folded up like bits of origami, unfold and grab on to one another when subjected to the stress of beating by whisk, creating bubble walls that then trap the air beaten into them. A form emerges. (Whites must be beaten without yolks, because yolks contain fats and lecithin that interfere with bubble bonding.)

In an oven, the form (and foam) rises, in accordance with Charles's law: when air heats, it expands; when it cools, it contracts. Water in the bubble walls changes from liquid to gas and it rises farther. Starch in flour or cocoa reinforces the strength of the bubble walls.

All this is psychologically calming. Anyone can ensure the rise of such a scientifically verified mixture, if not of his or her soul's.

Here is a recipe for a cheese soufflé. It closely follows one given to me by my friend Samin. All parts other than the beaten egg whites can be made earlier in the day, and left at room temperature, with the final beating and addition the only thing left for the end. This creates a handsome, if obvious, spectacle.

CHEESE SOUFFLÉ

6 tablespoons unsalted butter plus more for lining the mold
6 tablespoons all-purpose flour
1¼ cups whole milk
kosher salt
1¾ cups coarsely grated Gruyère or similar cheese
1¼ cups grated Parmesan cheese

4 eggs, separated
2 egg whites

Heat the oven to 425 degrees. Put a cookie sheet on the middle rack of your oven to help conduct heat evenly.

To make the béchamel, melt the butter, adding the flour as soon as it begins to foam, and mix well, then gradually add the milk, whisking the whole time as it comes to a boil. Once it thickens and bubbles, turn the heat as low as it will go and cook, stirring occasionally, for 10 to 15 minutes. Taste the béchamel and add salt, leaving it highly seasoned. Remove to a large bowl. Add the Gruyère and ¾ cup of the Parmesan to the béchamel. Once it is cool enough to touch, add the egg yolks, stirring or whisking them in one by one. Adjust the salt again, remembering that the finished soufflé will be twice this volume.

Butter a 1½- to 2-quart soufflé mold or other baking dish of a similar size and dust the inside with the remaining ½ cup Parmesan, tapping out the excess.

Beat all 6 egg whites just past soft peaks. Fold one-third of the whites into the soufflé base to lighten, then fold in the rest until fairly well combined, with large movements of the spatula, rotating the bowl and being careful not to overmix.

Pour the mixture into the prepared soufflé dish and set it on the cookie sheet on the middle rack in the oven. Lower the oven temperature to 400 degrees and bake for about 30 minutes, until puffed and just cooked inside, testing with a skewer or pressing for a just-firm top, which should be nicely browned.

In spring or summer, a wonderful addition is a half cup sliced spring garlic sautéed in butter, added to the béchamel as it cooks. This adds a green spring flavor, which is appealing.

If you cook a soufflé more slowly, its rise will be more modest, but its structure more stable. Such a soufflé can rise a second time, no matter what they say about such a phenomenon's unlikelihood. Particularly if you cook it in individual ramekins, then put the little soufflés back in the oven at dinnertime, they will puff up. This can also be made at the last moment and served immediately.

LEEK PUDDING SOUFFLÉ

9 to 10 cups halved and thinly sliced leeks (white and light green
    parts), washed well
8 tablespoons (1 stick) butter, plus more for the baking dish
3½ teaspoons plus ⅛ teaspoon kosher salt
4 tablespoons all-purpose flour
1 cup whole milk
½ cup grated Parmesan cheese
6 eggs, separated

*Sweat the leeks over medium heat in 6 tablespoons of the butter with 3½
teaspoons salt until just barely beginning to brown and totally dry, 10 to
15 minutes. Make a béchamel with the flour, remaining 2 tablespoons
butter, and the milk, following the directions on page 149 but cooking
for only 5 minutes. Remove from the heat. Add the Parmesan.*

Lightly butter a 1½-quart soufflé dish or loaf pan.

*In a blender, blend the leeks and béchamel until totally smooth. Add
the egg yolks, one or two at a time, until incorporated. Pour into a large
bowl.*

*Heat the oven to 300 degrees. Place a medium- to high-sided container
on a rack in the middle of the oven. Heat water in a kettle. Beat the egg
whites until they are just past soft peaks.*

*Gently fold the beaten egg whites into the leek-béchamel mixture,
then transfer to the prepared dish. Place the dish into the container in
the oven. Fill it, carefully avoiding splashing the soufflé, with 1 inch of
water. Cook for about 1½ hours, until the soufflé has risen significantly
and the top begins to brown nicely, and even crack, and feels just firm to
the touch. Let cool for a few minutes before serving, or if in individual
molds, let cool, then unmold, and at dinnertime, heat the oven to 400
degrees, drizzle lightly with cream, and place on a rack in the middle of
the oven. Once puffed, they are ready to serve.*

Or replace half the leeks with well-drained and finely chopped
spinach or butter-cooked celery root. Or omit any greens and make
a pudding soufflé of only cheese, experimenting with goat cheese,

with all the world's wondrous Tommes, with Reblochon, and with Roquefort, which makes a fine, fragrant, and distinctive variation. If it is warm, a soufflé is a meal, any cracks filled with vegetables that are ripe and good. A plate of bitter greens, like dandelion, makes a nice accompaniment. Or there can be a crisp green salad or, even better, an herb salad (page 75), or a succory salad (page 93) if you are hoping for luck in love, and ripe fruit and perhaps more cheese—a soft, fresh-tasting one—for dessert.

When the wind blows in gusts and guests are puffing at their hands, I serve soufflés as a first course, followed by garlic sausages and parsleyed potatoes, and then something soothing like brownies or wine-plumped figs and mascarpone or an apple crisp.

This is another kind of risen-egg dish yet. It is made in a shallower pan than a soufflé and rises less than the pudding soufflé on page 150. Its original recipe was written by Edna Lewis. Even with my small amendments, which make a country dish higher flown, it is fast and rustic, not the sort found in old classic French books, but in old American ones.

CORN PUDDING

5 tablespoons butter, plus more for pan
3 tablespoons all-purpose flour
2 cups whole milk
scant 1 cup grated Parmesan cheese
kosher salt
3 large eggs, separated
2 cups raw corn kernels (from 2 to 3 ears)
scant ½ teaspoon freshly grated nutmeg
freshly ground black pepper

Make a béchamel with 3 tablespoons butter, flour, and milk, following the directions on page 149. Cook for 20 minutes over the lowest possible heat. Remove from the heat. Add a heaping ½ cup of the Parmesan and season with salt. It should be quite highly seasoned. Cool until cool enough to touch.

*In a very hot pan, heat the remaining 2 tablespoons butter and cook
corn until hot and a little browned. Cool, off heat.*

*Heat the oven to 400 degrees. Butter a 9-inch, high-sided cake pan,
then coat lightly with remaining Parmesan, tapping out the excess.*

*Whisk the egg yolks into the béchamel mixture one by one. Mix in the
corn. Add the nutmeg judiciously (it should underline the dairy flavor
but not really be identifiable) and season with black pepper. Taste for
salt and adjust.*

*Beat the egg whites until they are just past soft peaks. Gently fold the
beaten egg whites into the béchamel mixture, then transfer the mixture
to the prepared baking dish. Set on a rack in the middle of the oven. Bake
for 25 to 30 minutes, until puffed and just cooked inside, which you can
check with a skewer or sharp knife.*

This should be floated down, not on "a fine old wine," but on good
cold light Pilsner and iced tea. I find this so honest and pure that I
append Brillat-Savarin's final notation on his tuna omelet: it should
be kept for gatherings of people "who appreciate what is served to
them and eat it thoughtfully and slowly." And, as he promised to his
deserving guests, miracles will happen.

Any risen pudding, whether a soufflé or one with a humbler rise,
is also an omelet. (In fact, the first soufflé, the *crème à la sultane*
published in Vincent La Chapelle's 1742 *Le Cuisinier Moderne,*
was truly just a raisin omelet whose whites were beaten separately
and top covered with sugar. And so they stayed, simply puffed-up
omelets, for about one hundred years . . .) In our house, any egg can
be any meal—except, usually, breakfast; every household must have
its quirks, and ours is to keep eggs for lunch or dinner. But, it can
hardly be denied that the egg preparation that makes eggs seem
most dignified is an omelet.

I have read that Gertrude Stein and Alice B. Toklas's cook, Helene,
demonstrated her antipathy toward the painter Henri Matisse by
declaring upon hearing he'd be staying for a meal: "In that case, I
will not make an omelet but fry the eggs. It takes the same number of
eggs and the same amount of butter, but it shows less respect, and he
will understand." I think it is not *which* egg preparation one chooses

but how dotingly one carries it out that makes or breaks a good meal of them. (Or in the case of eggs, breaks, then makes.)

Here is an omelet that is both respectful and simple. In Stein and Toklas's Paris, it would likely have been either turned into a soufflé, or into a folded French omelet, but I like it as a frittata.

A RESPECTFUL OMELET

½ pound thinnest green beans
1 teaspoon kosher salt, plus to taste
good olive oil
2 cloves spring garlic or 1 large clove cured garlic, pounded to a
    paste with a big pinch of salt
4 scallions, thinly sliced on an angle
1 to 2 tablespoons finely chopped fresh parsley
2 tablespoons finely chopped fresh marjoram
1 tablespoon lemon zest
½ to ⅔ cup finely chopped or pounded walnuts or pine nuts
12 eggs
¾ cup freshly grated Parmesan cheese
lemon wedges, for serving

Heat the oven to 375 degrees. Trim the stem end off the beans. Boil until tender in water salted to taste like seawater in 2 batches. Remove with a handheld sieve to cool on a baking sheet, drizzle liberally with good olive oil, then cut into bite-size pieces and mix along with a long pour of olive oil in a bowl with the garlic, scallions, herbs, zest, and nuts. Taste for salt and adjust. Beat the eggs in a large bowl with 1 teaspoon salt. Add the beans. Mix to combine.

Heat a 9- to 10-inch cast-iron pan over medium heat. Add enough olive oil to coat the pan well, then pour in the egg mixture. Move the mixture around to expose as much of it as possible to the bottom of the pan, then level the top. Once the sides are just set, which you can check with a spatula, put the pan in the oven and bake for 12 to 15 minutes, until the top is just firm. Remove from the oven and leave to cool for 1 minute. Invert onto a plate. After it has cooled for several minutes more, shower it with the cheese. Serve with lemon wedges.

A good variation is to add a half cup cooked zucchini along with the beans. In any season but summer, the *best* variation is to disregard my instruction for green beans, and instead use the same measurement of boiled potatoes and the pesto you shrewdly froze over the summer, or the dried spice mixture on which you rely when it is cold, mixed with olive oil and spread through the potatoes. Or cooked kale or spinach and handfuls of fresh dill, or turnips and an unexpected scrape of cinnamon. All make respectful omelets and, with chilled rosé or light red wine and warm baguette, respectable meals.

The painter Pontormo shared my view on eggs—perhaps because they are so round and luminous and seraphic. The diary he kept was mostly what he ate, and several entries show that as he sat, as broodily as the hens who made his meals, he survived on eggs: "Saturday night had supper with Piero, fish from the Arno, ricotta, eggs, and artichokes. Thursday night lettuce salad and caviar and an egg. Saturday went to the inn: salad and fish eggs and goat cheese and I felt well." He may have been broodier yet had he eaten the chicken, and was probably sustained by his temperance, if not his mercy.

In a generous mood, you might serve the bistro classic: eggs in red wine. These are also called, depending on the cookbook, *oeufs à la bourguignonne* or *oeufs en meurette*. By any name, they are among the most appetizing things ever to be made with eggs: two of them to a person, freshly poached, round and hot, soaked in a barely thickened redwine-and-broth sauce, garnished here and there with lardons of bacon and mushroom. The whole is dark and seductive and a little strange.

OEUFS EN MEURETTE

1 tablespoon olive oil
4 slices bacon or pancetta, cut into lardons
8 ounces any mushrooms, cleaned and sliced
1 clove garlic, lightly smashed
2 sprigs fresh thyme
kosher salt
2 cups chicken stock or beef stock
2 cups light red wine, like Gamay
1 bay leaf

4 tablespoons (½ stick) unsalted butter, plus a little more
1 tablespoon all-purpose flour
8 pieces peasant bread, toasted
a few drops of distilled white vinegar
8 good eggs
handful of chopped fresh parsley

Heat a frying pan. Add the olive oil, then the lardons, and cook over medium heat until just beginning to crisp. Remove with a slotted spoon. Add the mushrooms, garlic, and thyme. Cook until the mushrooms are dry. Salt lightly and turn off the heat; remove and discard the garlic. In a separate small pot, combine the stock, wine, and bay leaf. Cook over high heat until reduced by half. Add the mushrooms and season with salt.

Cut 2 tablespoons of the butter into cubes and coat lightly in the flour. Return the sauce to a simmer and whisk in the floured butter. Keep warm over the lowest heat.

Butter the toast and place 2 slices into each of four shallow bowls. Bring a shallow pan of water containing a few drops of vinegar to a bare simmer. Poach the eggs in rounds, breaking them first into individual ramekins before sliding them into the water. Remove with a slotted spoon to the waiting toasts, allotting 2 eggs per bowl.

Pour a small amount of the sauce around and over the eggs, lightly spooning mushrooms over each and topping with lardons. Top heavily with parsley and serve hot.

And why not do the same with white wine instead of red, and with butter-cooked leeks instead of mushrooms? Or with stout instead of any wine, and a great shaving of Gruyère or Gouda over the top of the eggs and their heady broth? That might call for a sprinkling of toasted rye seeds and a rough grind of black pepper over the top . . .

Is it irresponsible to provide only two egg-alone recipes in a book that means to revive old ways, when so many Cook Books from the last century (and the one before) had whole chapters on eggs, leaving the impression by iteration that eggs, carefully prepared, in tactful old ways like baked in cream, baked atop asparagus, and blanketed in Gruyère were the ingredient most able to rise to any occasion?

Then here are two more, maybe more poetic than practical.

I have, from Aldo Buzzi, a unique recipe for boiled eggs from Maestro Martino, a fifteenth-century chef from Como:

> *Eggs steeped in their shells* [Boiled eggs]: "Put the fresh eggs into cold water and allow them to boil for the duration of a Paternoster or a little longer."

And (I gloss) be given your bread, forgiven and forgiving, led from temptation and delivered to good, all before your toast soldiers are out of the oven.

And finally this nineteenth-century dish, which is really a drink. It may actually come in handy for those times when, as M.F.K. Fisher once wrote, "both man and egg are raw":

PRAIRIE OYSTER

1 quail's egg, raw and unbeaten
1 large slug whiskey
1 large slug strong beef broth
1 to 5 heavy shakes Tabasco

Leaving the yolk whole, combine all and drink it down quickly, the morning after—especially if you did not pray yesterday.

A FAST
AUTUMN DINNER

Vegetables à la grecque

Herbed crêpes with mushrooms

A plain green salad vinaigrette

Wine: A light red with sweet fruit,
a touch of smoke, and soft tannins
Example: Oregon Pinot Noir
Cristom Pinot Noir Mt. Jefferson Cuvée 2014

Orange blossom meringues

A GOOD EFFECT

Meat

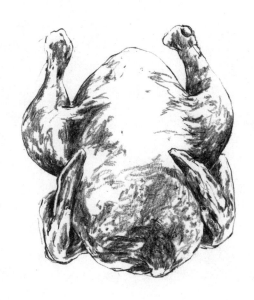

VI

When Art and Nature join, th'effect will be
Some nice ragout, or charming fricassee.
—William King, "The Art of Cookery"

I first read the word *fricassee* in a children's book, where it was part
of a rhyming device gone awry: "If at first, you can't fricassee, fry,
fry a hen." It doesn't even scan, the extra syllable in "fricassee" slowing
things down agitatingly . . . which is probably why it *sticks*.

The pun does educate its earwigged victim: To fricassee is *not* to
fry. Nor is it, for that matter, to stew, to brown, to poach, to broil, to
sauté, or to steam. To fricassee is to sauté ingredients in butter for a
while, counting on the butter to do an uncommon share of the labor
before doing or adding anything else.

That is the formal definition, anyway. In life as it is lived, fricassee
is also what anyone used to call a stew that possessed some culinary
conviction. As Julia Child wrote in 1961: "One frequently runs into
chicken recipes labeled sautés which are actually fricassees, and others
labeled fricassees which are actually stews. The fricassee is halfway
between the two." For at least half a century, in any case, one of the
most common dishes on American tables would have been *called* a
fricassee, no matter what it was.

I will risk criticism to assert that *fricassee* just means a small worth-
while fuss. Whether it is begun in olive oil or butter or mutton fat, if
one takes time with a pot of meat and vegetables, cooks it in careful
steps, leaving some parts aside for later addition, ending up with a dish
that is more delicate and arranged-tasting than the set-it-and-forget-it-
type stews that are today's standard, one has, to my mind, fricasseed.

This chicken fricassee comes from the vexations of pregnancy. I had made a fricassee for a party of robust eaters and drinkers—just the sort of group worth a small fuss—but, victim to waves of hormonal nausea, could not bring myself to eat anything but the dish's sauce and potatoes. Our guests copied me, out of a Victorian politesse, testifying eventually that chicken fricassee was better without chicken. I was hesitant to record this mutiny, but I continue to commit it. I boldly aver that the best chicken fricassee is a . . .

NOT-CHICKEN FRICASSEE

kosher salt
10 chicken wings
5 tablespoons butter
1 tablespoon olive oil
½ cup chopped carrots
½ cup diced celery
1 cup small-diced leeks, washed well
¾ cup dry white wine
8 ounces wild mushrooms, sliced or quartered
½ cup thinly sliced scallions
1 cup chicken broth
bouquet garni of thyme, parsley stems, a bay leaf
2 large egg yolks, at room temperature
¼ cup heavy cream
a squeeze of fresh lemon juice
3 tablespoons roughly chopped fresh tarragon
3 tablespoons roughly chopped fresh parsley

At least 3 hours before cooking, salt the chicken wings well and leave at room temperature.

Melt 4 tablespoons of butter in the olive oil in a large, deep, heavy-bottomed pan and brown the chicken wings in batches, and remove to a plate. (To serve the chicken as an appetizer, finish cooking: put, close together, in a roasting pan, for 30 minutes in a 375-degree oven.) Add the carrots, celery, leeks, and a sprinkle of salt to the empty pan, scraping the pan and using the vegetables to help it deglaze. Add a sprinkle of wine if needed. Cook until tender, 10 to 15 minutes. Add the mushrooms and scallions. Cook 1 to 2 minutes. Add the remaining wine and bring to a boil, stirring occasionally, until the liquid begins to reduce. Slowly add the broth, stirring, then the bouquet garni. Simmer 10 minutes. Meanwhile, whisk the yolks and cream in a separate bowl. Whisking, pour ½ cup fricassee sauce, slowly, into the yolk-cream mixture to temper it. Then slowly add all back into the pot. Remove the bouquet garni.

To serve, whisk the last tablespoon of butter into the fricassee and ladle into a warm platter, over fried or boiled potatoes, or buttered rice. Squeeze with lemon juice and scatter with herbs.

Perhaps you want chicken in your chicken fricassee. If so, replace the chicken wings with chicken thighs, still on their bones. Remove them as directed, as you would the chicken wings, after browning, and then return them to the pan to simmer as soon as the carrots, celery, and leeks have begun to cook. Add wine and broth and cook over medium-low heat for thirty minutes before adding the mushrooms and proceeding.

A fine addition to either meal is a cooked green, like spinach or dandelion or kale, and good bread, if you like, for wiping up the sauce.

Coq au vin was originally made of rooster, simmered into tastiness if not tenderness in wine, a provincial French home's most abundant resource. Following the pattern of an intuitive human behavior becoming a set of rules, this developed into authoritative precepts: coq au vin must have mushrooms, pearl onions, lardons of bacon, and good red wine.

I again rebel, not out of philosophic objection but pragmatism. I gather the mostly empty bottles of wine crowded into a counter corner, taking up space, take sips of each to make sure none has turned to vinegar, measure one to two cups, combine, and pour them into a pot to simmer with quickly browned chicken thighs and legs. The result leaves its submerged bird tasting as if it got taken to a party, saturated in the complexities of wine and a night on the town.

CHICKEN IN LEFTOVER WINE

kosher or sea salt
10 to 12 bone-in, skin-on chicken legs and thighs
3 to 4 tablespoons olive oil
1 cup chopped leeks, washed well, or onion
2 cups chopped fennel
1 cup chopped carrot
2 cloves garlic, unpeeled
bouquet garni of thyme stems, bay leaf, parsley stems, and
    rosemary
1 to 2 cups leftover wine
7 or 8 slices bacon, smoked or unsmoked, cut into ½-inch
    pieces
1 pound shallots, whole, peeled
1 pound mixed mushrooms, stemmed and sliced or
    quartered
large handful of chopped fresh parsley or celery leaves

Salt the chicken very well and leave at room temperature for 3 hours, or in the refrigerator overnight. Bring to room temperature, if refrigerated. Heat a large heavy pan. Add 3 tablespoons olive oil. Brown the skin-side of the chicken, 5 to 10 minutes, in batches, removing pieces as skin crisps to a waiting plate. Heat the oven to 325 degrees. Add the leeks, fennel, and carrot and stir, scraping up browned bits, with a wooden spoon. Cook over medium heat until the vegetables begin to soften, 3 to 5 minutes. Add the garlic cloves and bouquet garni. Add 1 cup wine, reserving ¼ to ½ cup for later, bring to a boil, then lower to a bare simmer. Nestle in the chicken. Place, uncovered, in the oven and cook until the meat is spoon tender, 40 to 60 minutes.

Meanwhile, render the bacon in a large, heavy pan. Once almost crisp, remove with a spoon to a bowl and add the shallot. Salt well, turning to brown lightly. Add drizzles of wine and water to cover by half and cook until just tender, 12 to 15 minutes. Remove from the pan, adding to reserved bacon, and return the pan to the heat. Add remaining olive oil, if needed, and mushrooms and cook without salt-

ing until lightly browned and cooked through. Salt to taste. Combine with the bacon and shallots. When the chicken is out of the oven, add the bacon, onions, and mushrooms and let sit together at room temperature 15 minutes to 1 hour. Just before eating, put under the broiler for 1 minute to ensure crisp skin. Shower heavily with herbs and serve.

This chicken in wine breaks with tradition in a handful of other ways, too: there is no flour or butter, but olive oil; there is less than half the wine as in the old recipes; if some of the wine was white and some red, the resulting sauce will have a blushing hue, strange enough to make the old masters faint, though not unappetizing to me. But it is literally chicken *au vin*, which I hope makes it defensible.

My father had strong and eccentric tastes. He breakfasted on tins of sardines, boiled eggs, and avocados, ate pickles at every meal, and lunched on potent highballs of vodka and orange juice and pistachios. But he would not eat a fish with bones, and he refused anything containing cooked celery. I, who love the crisp simplicity of raw celery—though not nearly as much as I loved my father—grew up professing that I, too, despised it cooked. In truth, I may have liked cooked celery then, and very much like it now. I find, moreover, that I often *have* celery, which recommends it as an ingredient. Its presence led me, one day, to this primitive variation on Xavier Raskin's chicken *à la Montmorency* from his stout and indispensable 1922 *The French Chef in Private American Families: A Book of Recipes.*

CHICKEN À LA MONTMORENCY

kosher salt
1 (3-pound) chicken, cut into 12 pieces
2 ounces or 3 slices fatty bacon or pancetta, cut into large pieces
2 tablespoons unsalted butter
2 bunches scallions, cleaned and cut into 2-inch pieces
2 cups celery that has been halved lengthwise then cut into
    2-inch pieces
¾ to 1 cup water
sherry or leftover wine

Salt the chicken very well and leave at room temperature for 3 hours, or in the refrigerator overnight. Bring to room temperature, if refrigerated. Crisp the bacon in the butter. Remove the bacon, leaving all the fat behind. Brown the skin-side of the chicken, keeping heat low enough to avoid browning the butter much, 5 to 10 minutes, removing pieces as skin crisps, to a waiting plate. Add the scallions, celery, water, and a splash of sherry. Return all the chicken, skin up, and cover. Cook over low heat about 10 minutes. Check and remove the white meat. Re-cover and continue cooking over low heat, another 20 to 30 minutes or until the dark meat is done. Return the white meat to the pan, along with the bacon. Sprinkle again lightly with sherry, heat through and serve.

In spring and summer, this benefits from wedges of little Tokyo turnips, with some of their tender greens still attached, added toward the end of cooking and turned a few times in the chicken's juices. Small tufts of watercress can also be added a few minutes before the end, giving the whole dish a rivery feel. This is good with white rice or *riz à la Georgienne*. A bowl of warm lentils makes a sturdy third leg.

James Beard called chicken Kiev a "Russian Specialty." The Russian Tea Room claims it was invented by Antoine Carême for a tsar—and so is French with Russian ornamentations. I do not know what the Russians themselves believe. I assume it is that chicken Kiev, along with tea, ballet, and space exploration, was invented by them.

In its original form, chicken Kiev was a chicken breast rolled around herb butter, secured by toothpicks, breaded, and fried. I have ruminated, while rolling and breading and freezing, on the question of whether, in order to *be* chicken Kiev, the dish must be so much trouble. One must freeze the butter, then freeze the stuffed breasts to avoid their incurring a (rather common) leak.

I have proven in the unscientific laboratory of my own kitchen that the pleasure in eating chicken Kiev lies not in the deception and surprise of its butter remaining hidden and making a grand entrance but in how good fried chicken is with herb butter.

I am certain it is simpler, and I believe it as good, to mix fresh herbs into sweet butter, fry chicken breasts until crisp, and then smear them with the ruddy green butter, which will start to melt in lovely pools that instant. This can be thought of as . . .

CHICKEN KIEV, OF A KIND

2 chicken breasts
kosher salt
optional: freshly ground black pepper
4 tablespoons (½ stick) unsalted butter, at room temperature
½ clove garlic, pounded to a paste with a tiny bit of salt
1 tablespoon finely chopped scallion
2 tablespoons finely chopped fresh parsley

1 tablespoon fresh tarragon, finely chopped
a few drops of fresh lemon juice
1 cup all-purpose flour
2 eggs, beaten
soft white breadcrumbs or panko breadcrumbs
vegetable or grapeseed oil, for frying

Pull off the chicken tenders and reserve them, or include, and lightly pound each breast with a rolling pin to even out its thickness, then cut each in half. Season each well with salt and black pepper, if you like. Leave at room temperature for 30 minutes, or refrigerate for 2 to 3 hours.

Combine the butter, garlic, scallion, parsley, tarragon, and lemon juice and mash to make herb butter, then season with salt. Form into a cylinder and refrigerate or leave in a bowl at room temperature.

Put the flour, eggs, and breadcrumbs into three separate shallow dishes. Set a draining rack over a cookie sheet at the far side of the three. Dip the chicken pieces first in the flour, then in the egg, then in the breadcrumbs, shaking off any excess of each. Set the breaded chicken on the rack as you finish each piece. In a large, deep pan, heat ¾ to 1 inch of vegetable oil to 375 degrees, or until a breadcrumb dropped into the hot oil fries to golden in about 15 seconds. If there is room in the pan to leave nearly an inch between the pieces of chicken, fry them all at once. Otherwise, fry them in two batches. Cook for 4 to 5 minutes per side, adjusting the heat to keep the frying steady.

Remove each briefly to the cleaned rack for a moment. Serve hot, with a lot of cold herb butter on each.

Anything goes with these crisp, buttery fillets, and nothing but a salad is needed. If there is anything left after dinner, it should tomorrow be made automatically into sandwiches with mayonnaise, tufts of herbs, and olive oil.

The words *deviled chicken* have always suggested to me elaborate picnics packed in hampers, watered by Champagne, accompanied by fresh rolls, followed by wild strawberries. But the deviled chicken recipes I have tried have revealed the evocative "deviling" that sparked such imaginative interest to be nothing but an illusory name for adding paprika, mustard, and sometimes breadcrumbs—all possessing a certain piquancy, but not *devilish*. Here is what I wanted deviled chicken to be. It is, if not infernally spicy, at least purgatorially so, and best cold, the day after making it, packed into a hamper and—if you have the knees for it—eaten in the grass.

COLD DEVILED CHICKEN

FOR THE MARINADE

⅔ cup whole-milk yogurt

⅔ cup smooth Dijon mustard

6 tablespoons Tabasco

½ cup beer

2 teaspoons Colman's dried mustard

2 teaspoons ground cayenne

4 teaspoons spicy paprika

4 tablespoons (½ stick) butter, at room temperature

5 tablespoons kosher salt

a lot of freshly ground black pepper

4 pounds bone-in, skin-on chicken thighs

2 to 3 tablespoons vegetable oil

Mix all the marinade ingredients in a bowl. Add the chicken and mix well. Marinate overnight in the refrigerator, or for up to 2 nights.

Heat the oven to 375 degrees. Wipe the marinade from the chicken. Heat a heavy oven-safe pan to hot but not smoking. Add the oil. Add the chicken, skin side down. Working in batches if needed, cook over medium-high heat, rotating the pan occasionally to brown all sides, until the skin is deep caramel brown, 5 to 7 minutes.

Return all the thighs to the pan, skin side down, and place in the oven. Bake for 10 minutes. Remove, flip the pieces, and lower the oven temperature to 350 degrees. Bake for 25 to 30 minutes more, until the thighs are completely tender. Let cool in the refrigerator and serve cool.

This is a perfect picnic dish, a fine companion to potato rolls and cabbage salad, and a delicious lunch indoors.

Thinking of old-fashioned picnics and lunches—or luncheons— one is naturally led by a thematic rope to jellied chicken, also called: chicken in *chaud-froid*, marbled chicken, *poulet en gelée, poularde froide a l'estragon*, and *poularde à la gelée à l'estragon* . . . and dozens of dainty names referring to a delicate dish that was probably for a hundred years or more the most successful exercise of Victorian decorum.

It is not, in general, a success today. Appearances aside—for jellied chicken is very beautiful—it cannot be denied that chicken has a number of natural textures already very like jelly. This can make eating *poulet en gelée* a practice in overstatement, with one jelled texture insisting itself upon another.

Cool, though, is a temperature that has a wonderfully concentrating effect on a good chicken's own flavors. I recommend, therefore, cooking a chicken as though to make a jelly of it—slowly poaching it in water or broth to which you have added star anise, verdant coriander, black pepper, and fennel, and then never bothering about the jelly and serving it chilled.

I find homemade mayonnaise to be a perfect foil to this slightly enigmatic chilled fowl. The result is just similar enough to *gelées* for me to feel I'm not burning tradition on the pyre of progress. The resulting broth, from which jelly *would* have been made, is the start of a dozen dishes, only a fraction of them soup, which my frugal soul appreciates.

POACHED CHICKEN MAYONNAISE

FOR THE CHICKEN
kosher salt
1 (3- to 4-pound) heritage breed chicken
½ carrot
2 stalks fennel
½ stalk celery
1 leek top or onion skin
2 cloves garlic, unpeeled
1 bay leaf

handful of parsley stems
1 star anise pod
a few whole coriander seeds
a few whole black peppercorns
water or homemade chicken stock

FOR THE MAYONNAISE
2 egg yolks, from room-temperature eggs
1 dab of smooth Dijon mustard
2 cups very good olive oil
a squeeze of fresh lemon juice
a few drops room-temperature water
a drop of red wine vinegar
¾ teaspoon kosher salt, plus to taste

Salt the chicken three times as heavily as you feel comfortable doing and leave it, uncovered, in the refrigerator overnight. The following day, bring it to room temperature. Put the carrot, fennel, celery, leek top, garlic, bay leaf, parsley stems, and spices, tied in bundles, if you like, and chicken in a pot that fits all the ingredients closely. Cover with water by about ½ inch. Bring to a boil, then lower to below a simmer, skimming any scum that rises with the boil. Cook for 30 to 60 minutes, depending on the size of the chicken, until a leg wiggles easily and the juices inside run just clear.

Remove the chicken to a plate and let cool. Strain the broth and refrigerate or freeze it for future use. Let the chicken sit at room temperature, uncovered, until ready to eat.

To make the mayonnaise, whisk the egg yolks with the mustard until uniform, then add the majority of the olive oil, drop by drop. Once the mayonnaise emulsifies, add a little lemon juice, then add the remaining oil in a very light stream, and a few drops of water when it gets thick. Add a drop of red wine vinegar at the end. Taste and season with salt. Refrigerate until ready to serve.

To serve, arrange the carved chicken—boneless breasts cut into slices, legs and thighs divided, bone-in—on a platter with the mayonnaise in a deep bowl in the middle. Encourage ample use of mayonnaise as a sauce, perhaps demonstrating by example.

A good variation is to add a clove of garlic, pounded to a paste with a little salt to the mayonnaise, producing the Provençal sauce aïoli. Another is to add ½ cup fresh parsley, tarragon, or chervil, which will lend a delightfully herbal strain, or two or three threads of saffron, staining the sauce a flamboyant orange and rendering it even more lustrous.

This is a truly fine alternative to that serially loved and overestimated preparation of the bird as it is usually eaten today: hot. But if cold fowl is too enigmatic for you, it is good warm. It can then safely go by the name *poulet au pot*, once heartily desired by Henry IV for his subjects and zealously promised by Herbert Hoover to his, and notably delivered by neither.

There is for every person an ingredient or a cooking process from which he or she shies—the one *thing* in a dish or recipe that causes him or her to withdraw.

I observe it in myself when a recipe starts with boiling sugar for caramel, or demands a candy thermometer (or *any* thermometer). I know many other people who are happy taking ingredients' temperatures but cannot abide the texture of jelly (I hope they will try chilled chicken and not be themselves too chilled by prefatory mention of jellied chicken . . .). And more yet who get spontaneous shivers at dishes containing a lot of what we indiscriminately call *fat*. I am ill-equipped to deal with their therapy, having my own prejudices, but none against fat. I love duck fat and cream used judiciously. I will soak anything, including myself, in olive oil, if it is good.

I admit, though, that many canonical recipes by Pierre Franey and Craig Claiborne and Julia Child, and earlier, by Ranhofer, Ali-Bab, and Escoffier, whatever they are nominally *for*, yield dishes tasting of . . . butter and cream, cream and butter, whether the underlying ingredient is an egg or a chicken or something less allegorical. This exacerbates a problem: if a cook who shrinks from butter or cream timidly experiments, she will keep her prejudices because her dinner was too rich.

This is a particular problem concerning chicken cooked in cream, a dish too good to miss. My favorite version is Julia Child's *suprêmes de volaille aux champignons* (chicken breasts with mushrooms in cream), which calls for chicken breasts turned quite completely in butter, briefly covered in wax paper, and then soaked in cream and . . . that's it. It is so gentle that it brings to mind Chinese and Vietnamese chicken poaching, where delicate meat is coaxed into doneness off-heat. When lightly tossed with fresh spring onions wilted in melted butter, allowed a few moments to finish cooking in its own juices, and sauced with a drizzle of cream, buttery mushrooms, and fresh herbs, such a *suprême* is a unique delight.

SUPRÊMES DE VOLAILLE AUX CHAMPIGNONS

4 boneless, skinless chicken breast fillets, tenders pulled off
kosher salt
5 tablespoons unsalted butter, plus more as needed
2 tablespoons minced scallion or spring onion
8 ounces mushrooms, sliced
¼ cup chicken stock
1 tablespoon wine
2 tablespoons heavy cream
2 tablespoons chopped fresh parsley, chervil, or chives

Season the breasts and tenders heavily with salt. Leave at room temperature for 20 minutes. Heat the oven to 400 degrees. Melt the butter in a heavy, oven-safe casserole with a lid, large enough to hold the chicken in a single layer. Add the scallion and sauté for a moment without browning. Add the mushrooms and cook for 2 to 3 minutes. Roll the chicken into the onion-mushroom mixture and lay a piece of buttered wax paper cut to fit the pot directly over it. Cover the pot and place into the oven. In 6 minutes, press the chicken with your finger. From Child: "If still soft, return to oven for a moment or two. When the meat is springy to the touch it is done." Remove the chicken to a plate and cover lightly with aluminum foil. Move the casserole to the stovetop and turn the heat underneath it to medium-high. Cook the mushrooms for 3 minutes more. Once dry, season lightly with salt. Add the stock and wine and bring to a boil. When you can no longer smell the wine, add the cream. Cook for another 30 seconds. Add half the herbs. Taste for salt and adjust. Turn

off the heat. Return the chicken briefly to the pot and turn it in the sauce.
Remove to a platter, add the remaining herbs, and serve at once.

It is vital to really listen to Julia. The chicken breasts should be removed from the low heat the very *instant* they are cooked, or seconds before. A chicken breast that is truly *just* cooked through is a wondrous thing—tender, almost delicate, bearing no resemblance to the hard-to-chew resilient articles that come off grills all spring and summer.

I have tried several times to make versions of this dish with bone-in cuts of chicken, or with small chickens, cut in halves, all of which looked beautiful and very promising upon the plate. Alas, the results repeatedly brought to mind a notation of Ludwig Bemelmans's from a 1964 meal at the great Pyramide: "The chicken we were served was cooked in cream, flavored with estragon, and it was so-so—."

Depending on whether you trust Alexandre Dumas, Waverley Root, the American Poultry Association, or another source, there are somewhere more than forty and maybe more than sixty varieties of duck, about which once wafted an air of accessible luxury. Nineteenth-century women cooked duck because their men hunted it, especially the once ubiquitous canvasback, which they say tasted of wild celery. By the second half of the twentieth century, ducks came from farms on Long Island, were the big, fatty Peking, and had become a less obvious thing to cook.

One duck dish—duck à l'orange—was, however, not only on the menu of every Anglo-Americo-Franco restaurant, but as common at dinner parties, probably until 1970, as cheese and crackers. Some cooks probably followed Julia Child's three-page recipe for roasted Long Island ducklings with orange-scented, arrowroot-thickened glacé. Many others relied on quick mash-ups of canned bouillon mixed with marmalade poured over duck breast in innocent mangling.

Here is an alternative relying on duck legs cooked in duck fat, called duck confit, instead of on the somewhat technical, messy, and time-consuming process of roasting a whole duck. The confited legs can be made days or weeks ahead, or bought at many butchers. The sauce is a fruity, rustic broth, good for soaking potatoes in. This is startlingly good.

DUCK CONFIT À L'ORANGE

FOR THE CONFIT
¼ cup chopped fresh parsley leaves
1 tablespoon chopped fresh sage leaves
⅛ teaspoon fennel seeds
1 juniper berry
2 bay leaves, hard stem removed
a few black peppercorns
3 tablespoons kosher salt
6 duck legs
4 to 5 cups duck fat or a combination of duck fat and olive oil

FOR THE ORANGE SAUCE
12 cups poultry broth
¼ cup sherry vinegar, plus to taste
julienned peel of 3 oranges
1 to 1½ cups fresh orange juice
suprêmed sections of 5 or 6 oranges
3 tablespoons sugar
kosher salt
9 tablespoons unsalted butter, cubed

To confit the duck legs, in a spice grinder or mortar, pound together the parsley, sage, fennel seeds, juniper, bay leaves, peppercorns, and salt. Cut around the ankle bone of the legs and remove any thick, wobbly, excess fat. Season the legs heavily with spiced salt—a heavy snowfall on the skin side, lighter on the meat side. You will have a few spoonfuls left, unless the legs are monstrous, but better too much than too little. Save and use for seasoning steak. Refrigerate, covered, overnight. The next day, brush any visible salt and bring to room temperature. Heat the oven to 250 degrees. Melt the duck fat. Carefully place the duck legs in a single layer, skin side up, in an oven-safe casserole, submerging them completely. Cover tightly with aluminum foil and place in the oven for 3 to 5 hours, or until a knife slides easily in and out of a leg. Remove from the oven and remove the

duck legs from the fat. (Once cool, you can resubmerge the legs and store
them in the refrigerator, covered in the fat, for up to 1 month.)

To make the orange sauce, bring the broth to a boil and cook until it
has reduced by half. Add the vinegar, orange peel, orange juice, orange
sections, and sugar. Reduce over medium-high heat until the sauce coats
a spoon lightly. Taste and adjust the salt and vinegar. Just before serving,
whisk in the butter, bit by bit.

To serve, heat the oven to 375 degrees. Warm in the oven, skin side
up, then crisp the confit, skin side down, in a hot pan. Serve on a warm
platter with the sauce poured over.

You can also use duck legs someone has confited for you. In that
case, preparation will have been a fast affair, and you might take the
time to boil little potatoes and fry them in the duck fat in which your
confit was packed (page 109). This is also delicious with frisée salad
dressed with a sprinkle of vinegar and some of the delicious sauce,
and perhaps some warm lentils or stewed spiced chickpeas.

Based on how much most humans think they like change and how
little they actually do, I suspect that anyone who ate duck à l'orange as
a child will find my sauce thin. I cannot change my own taste. James
Beard's flour-thickened orange sauce and Julia Child's arrowroot-
thickened one both taste sticky to me. I am bound by honesty to my
brothy version, to which flour or arrowroot can be added, if they are
to your taste.

If, on the other hand, adding a finicky sauce to rustic, provincial

duck confit—which you know can be eaten plain, with country wine, coarse bread, and coarser conversation—seems like culinary voodoo, make only the confit, keep it in its fat, and crisp it when you are in the mood, serving it with a fast combination of orange zest, chopped parsley, and garlic, or as they do in Gascony, over tender beans with gizzards also cooked in fat, and enough wine to wash the morose and delicious affair down.

If my commitment to lost recipes were comprehensive, I would give ten more duck recipes: for duck with sour cherries, duck with macadamia nuts and sage, and duck soup—though I might here, to satisfy my childish sense of humor, provide the Marx brothers': "Take two turkeys, one goose, four cabbages, but no duck, and mix them together . . ." Then, having provided a small, solid foundation for my belief that birds other than chickens (and the annual procedural turkey) can be successfully cooked at home, I would firmly move on to recipes for roast squab and roast guinea hen with their own rustic sauces, subtly strengthening my case.

But I can't be comprehensive. So instead I will be bold. Here is my favorite recipe for a bird that is not a chicken. Freshly grilled little quails, steeped in sherry and served atop crisp canapés, are surely one of the most delicate and sustaining of nineteenth- and mid-twentieth-century offerings. They deserve a special place. As Alexandre Dumas once said (of English beefsteaks), there is "nothing to compare with them for exciting the appetite." A little burnished bird on a tiny, pâté-topped toast . . . how fussy . . . and how tantalizing. In truth, the dish is small but filling, and doesn't only excite the appetite but satisfy it.

GRILLED QUAILS ON CANAPÉS

4 quails
¼ cup diced spring onion
¼ cup minced green garlic, plus 3 tablespoons minced green
    garlic or 1½ tablespoons minced regular garlic
1 bay leaf, crumbled
3 tablespoons dry sherry
1½ teaspoons kosher salt, plus to taste

4 tablespoons good olive oil, plus more for the toast
3 tablespoons butter
8 ounces wild mushrooms, sliced
½ cup sliced shallot or spring onion
4 (½-inch-thick) slices peasant bread
1 recipe Chicken liver à la Toscane (page 18), or any simple
    chicken liver pâté
3 tablespoons chopped fresh parsley

Bone the quails except for the drumsticks and the last part of the wing
bones. (This is easy once you've watched a video.) In a food processor or
using a mortar and pestle, combine the spring onion, 3 tablespoons green
garlic, the bay leaf, sherry, and salt into a rough marinade. Stir in 3
tablespoons of the olive oil and marinate the quails at room temperature
for 2 to 3 hours or in the refrigerator overnight.

Heat a large heavy pan. Melt the butter with the remaining 1 tablespoon olive oil and add the mushrooms and shallot. Cook, stirring, until
both wilt, then add the remaining ¼ cup garlic. Cook until the mushrooms have released all their liquid. Once they begin to brown, salt to
taste and turn off the heat. Leave the mushrooms in the pan.

Lightly drizzle the bread with olive oil. Heat a grill or cast-iron pan.
Remove the quails from the marinade and grill over high heat for 2 to 3
minutes per side, basting with the marinade. Flip a final time and cook
for 2 to 3 minutes more. Remove to rest. While the quails rest, grill or
toast the bread, oil side down, leaving one side un-grilled. Remove to
plates and spread the grilled side thickly and evenly with the pâté. Briefly
reheat the mushrooms and add the parsley. Remove the quails, still hot,
to the pâté-topped toasts. Spoon mushrooms over each quail.

I find some nebulous holiness in the gastronomic paganism that
turns the fine, pink livers of some birds into pâté, meat into dinner . . .
and (I muse) feathers into a new autumn cap. The best accompaniment to such a compact feast is, appropriately, a salad of harsh,
wild-tasting greens. A salad of these, alongside a toast and a quail, is
a timeless pleasure and a kind of natural prayer.

I have been urged, but refuse, to include a recipe for the calf's liver so often served to yesteryear's children for good health. I am not among those who would rather face hunger than an animal's head, tongue, tail, lights, livers, knuckles, or feet. I love chicken livers and duck and goose livers, and have dined in festive bliss on what are called in their native languages *tête de veau* and *tête de cochon*. But I do not like to cook or eat the livers of cows, and so can't help the recipes for them that moan to be revived. I continue to *taste* them, in which I see some spiritual sense.

The transition is easy from liver to raw beef, which I credit with strengthening my spine, if not my *spiritus*, more times than I can count.

I had four places I used to go for beef tartare when I lived in Manhattan. Each was a little different: One used a quail's egg instead of a hen's egg. One served *pommes gaufrettes* instead of toast. The third served bread grilled over coal. My favorite was a dark, expansive North African–French bistro, where an order of tartare arrived as a great, unmixed mound of cold raw beef with mustard, onion, caper, anchovy, cornichon, and egg in little bowls, and slim, crisp French fries alongside. The restaurant wasn't reputable, and I shouldn't have felt secure ordering raw meat. And yet, I did. The air smelled good, the windows were always open, and the tartare tasted clean and pure, as though the chef loved the dish and made his concessions elsewhere.

I maintain Galenic views about dietary sympathy where the bodies of animal and man are concerned: we are what we eat. The beef for tartare should be from a cow who ate grass. It should be bought from someone who knows that the creature had a good clean bed, pleasant company, and a life relatively free of illness and hardship. Its meat will taste better and the alternatives, especially uncooked, could kill you. Also, the beef must be kept cold and the egg only cool—a very cold raw egg is as unappetizing as warm raw beef.

I agree with others who have called this dish somewhat barbarous. But if eaten with good cheer, gratitude, and good potato chips, it is also a reminder of the basically simple state in which we all live. Here is the steak tartare I make, when the right conditions are met, and that reminder hoped for.

STEAK TARTARE

8 ounces grass-fed filet mignon, cleaned of all silver skin and
   tendon
¼ teaspoon Worchestershire sauce
5 or 6 shakes of Tabasco
2½ anchovy fillets, minced
1 tablespoon capers, chopped
2 tablespoons minced red onion, soaked in ice water and drained
1 tablespoon minced fresh parsley
1 teaspoon smooth Dijon mustard
1 tablespoon olive oil
¼ to ½ teaspoon kosher salt, or to taste
freshly ground black pepper
2 egg yolks
potato chips or white toast and lettuce salad, for serving

*Place the steak in the freezer for 20 minutes to make it easier to chop.
Chop it neatly and finely—into slices, then matchsticks, and then tiny
cubes—and chill for 10 minutes more. Quickly add the remaining ingredients except for the egg yolks. Serve mounded on individual plates with
a yolk on top of each mound, and potato chips or white toast and lettuce
salad.*

The recipe is written for only two. I have never made beef tartare
for a greater number. Whatever it is that makes beef tartare barbaric
also makes it intimate, and though one certainly *could* serve it to
more, I never have.

The Vicomte de Mauduit claimed that raw beef could be used to
cure warts. I don't know if it works, or if you would stoop so low
(nor if the outcome is affected by the beef having been mixed with
mustard and caper). But perhaps you are desperate, and welcome the
knowledge that the remedy has been tried.

Maybe less tiresomely, though it depends on circumstance, leftover
tartare can be formed into a patty, placed in a hot cast-iron pan or
grill, and eaten as a hamburger.

Indeed, it is wise, for the body and soul, to sometimes reverse course and eat your beef cooked.

Salisbury steak originated as hand-chopped sirloin formed into a steak and cooked in butter. It existed on the menus of fine Swiss and French restaurants here and in their native lands as *bifsteak haché*, *Hamburg steak*, or *haché de boeuf*. The innocent mixture appeared under its new name in 1888, for a recipe by a Dr. Salisbury, consisting of chopped meat, seasoned with Worcestershire sauce and mustard, and griddled. How many times it was re-created in that naïve form I don't know. By 1962, according to a book I have from that year, titled *Meats*, and a number of similar editions, recipes for Salisbury steak had become burial grounds for convenience foods. The one in *Meats* reads: "1 lb. ground beef, ½ cup evaporated milk . . . flour, margarine . . . Worcestershire sauce . . . 1 4 oz. can mushrooms, undrained . . ." (This is succeeded by a recipe for Savory Beef Burgers that begins: "1½ cups Rice Krispies . . .")

Good hamburgers are delicious without their buns, and there are many ways to lift them up without condensed milk or Rice Krispies. In a 1982 recipe for the *New York Times,* Pierre Franey called for ground sirloin mixed with Gorgonzola cheese, flattened into patties and griddled in cast iron before a flaming in cognac—one can almost hear the opening bars of "La Marseillaise" through the blue flames. Perhaps my favorite chopped steak (which is what *steak haché* means) is another by Pierre Franey, in the *Chicago Tribune*, called "Steak hache (hamburger) with an egg rider." One grills sirloin patties, fries one egg per, and tops the burgers with them, then lays anchovy fillets around the yolks of the freshly cooked eggs. Then one sizzles a handful of capers and chopped parsley in hot butter and pours it over each beef-and-egg-and-anchovy stack. (In a flash of heathen inspiration, I devised a thuggish inversion of Franey's method, cooking a small, fatty sirloin patty quickly until well browned outside and still almost bloody within. I then pour all the fatty juices from the pan over a halved, lightly boiled egg. The hot juices cook the egg a bit further, and marinate and warm it. I eat the egg and sirloin together over a mix of young lettuces, thinking: *Now* this *is a fine way to eat steak and eggs!*)

Another good variation goes by its Italian name, *svizzerina*, at the little Via Carota in Greenwich Village, and consists of hand-chopped sirloin steak, salt, and pepper, cooked in olive oil with a single clove of garlic.

Here is a contribution to the category by my husband, Peter, who keeps the midcentury habit of mushrooms. There is some finicky deftness to his adorning of the dish with two sauces. Though I wouldn't have devised the rule, I obey it.

MON PIERRE'S STEAK HACHÉ

1 cup dried porcini mushrooms
1 pound best ground sirloin or chuck
5½ tablespoons butter, at room temperature
3 tablespoons finely chopped white onion
1 egg, beaten
kosher salt
3 tablespoons freshly grated Parmesan cheese
1 tablespoon red wine vinegar

½ teaspoon capers, finely chopped
½ cup finely chopped fresh parsley
olive oil

*Soak the mushrooms in boiling water for 20 minutes, then drain through
a fine-mesh sieve set over a bowl and finely chop; reserve the soaking
liquid. In a medium bowl, mix the beef, 5 to 6 tablespoons of the mushrooms, 1½ tablespoons of the butter, 1 tablespoon of the onion, the egg,
a large pinch of salt, and the Parmesan until well combined. Form into
four patties.*

*Make porcini butter by combining the remaining mushrooms and 4
tablespoons butter and a sprinkle of salt. Make salsa verde by soaking the
remaining onion in the vinegar with a sprinkle of salt for 10 minutes,
then adding the capers, parsley, and olive oil to make it a bit swimmy;
taste for salt and adjust.*

*Heat a heavy cast-iron pan and drizzle with olive oil. Cook the
chopped steaks for 4 minutes on the first side, salting them liberally. Flip
and cook for 4 minutes on the second side, salting again. (Cook longer
for medium.) Remove the steaks to a waiting hot plate. Top immediately
with the porcini butter. Let rest a few moments, then spoon salsa verde
over each and serve.*

It goes without saying—or perhaps more correctly, I have already
said—that these buttered, herby chopped steaks do not need buns.
Nor do they need the mechanical partnership of potatoes. They look
and taste as good accompanied by buttery rice or a chicory salad as by
spuds. If you do want your meat and potatoes to *be* meat and potatoes,
the fried ones on page 109 are particularly fine.

It has been years since we have appreciated our richesse in beef and
butter and cream. Steaks, though not good ones, can be bought for a
few dollars at a standard supermarket. Hamburgers and milk shakes
provide daily access to the bland luxury once breathlessly epitomized
in the boozy dish inspired by the huntress Diana: steak Diane.

Steak Diane, the rare classic delicacy that is not French but American, was born here . . . and it died here. Moreover I have made enough
adjustments to the original to set the ghosts of last century (and maybe

even of Diana herself) turning in their graves. But after repeating the traditional method a number of times, I found it irrevocably lifeless. I made changes, and it resurrected itself with the conviction and almost holy spontaneity of Lazarus. I think of this as:

STEAK DIANE HALLELUJAH!

12 ounces good strip steak or filet mignon
kosher salt
1½ teaspoons coarsely ground black peppercorns
½ teaspoon coarsely ground Sichuan peppercorns
½ teaspoon fennel seeds, coarsely ground
½ teaspoon coriander seeds, coarsely ground
1 tablespoon olive oil
3 tablespoons unsalted butter
¼ cup finely minced shallots
3 tablespoons cognac
1 teaspoon smooth Dijon mustard
a few drops of Worcestershire sauce
½ cup chicken stock
¼ cup crème fraîche
handful of roughly chopped fresh parsley

Clean the steak of all fat and divide it into two portions. Lightly pound each with a rolling pin or wine bottle to about ¾ inch thick. Salt well. Combine the peppercorns and spices. Coat the steaks well with the mixture and leave at room temperature for 20 minutes. Collect the other ingredients near the stove.

Heat a large, heavy-bottomed pan. Add the olive oil and half the butter. As soon as the butter sizzles, add the steaks, at medium heat so the meat sizzles mid-energetically. Cook for 1½ to 2 minutes, until the first side is caramelized and brown, then flip and cook the second side. Remove to a nearby plate. Add the remaining butter, turning the heat low. Add the shallots and a pinch of salt. Cook until the shallots are just translucent, 2 to 3 minutes. Turn the heat to high, add the cognac, and step back while it ignites and burns out. Again lower the heat, add the mustard and Worcestershire, and stir, then add the stock. Cook for 1 to 2 minutes, until it is a little reduced and tastes good, then add the crème fraîche, cook for 1 minute, and add the steaks, turning with a spoon once or twice to finish cooking in the sauce, 1 to 2 minutes. Remove the steaks to plates; add the parsley to the sauce and pour the sauce over the meat.

This is also for two, for economic reasons. It is as easy to make for four, almost as easy for six, and challenging but doable for eight. It is delicious with Italian creamed spinach, page 117. A few leaves of lemon-and-oil-dressed endive alongside also provide brightness and crunch.

If Steak Diane hallelujah adds strong flavors to good steak, beef braised in water relies on the good flavor of beef alone. I imagine the early incarnations of such a plain preparation were rough and hardly edible affairs. But if a fine chuck is well seasoned and treated carefully, the result is a tender flavorful roast and a broth that is the essence of beef. It may be a simplistic replacement for *boeuf au sauce Mornay, boeuf au sauce béarnaise, boeuf bercy, à la bordelaise, marchand de vins, chausseur, Henri IV* . . . which cycled in constant succession through fine menus in years past. But I think it is an improvement.

I hoped to compensate for the humble treatment of the beef by adorning it with traditional *sauce piquante*, made by boiling shallot in vinegar then adding cooking liquid from braised beef, adding that to béchamel, and finishing it with capers, cornichons, parsley, chervil, and tarragon. But my insides revolted against the richness of the béchamel in a supposedly piquant sauce. So this dish's suggested sauces are humble, too.

BEEF BOUILLI

kosher salt
1 (4-pound) chuck eye roast
2 stalks fennel
2 leek tops
1 carrot
1 stalk celery

stems from ½ bunch parsley
1 star anise pod
2 bay leaves
2 cloves garlic, unpeeled
anchovy butter, herb butter, porcini butter, or salsa verde (pages
        38 and 183) and flaky salt, for serving

Salt the chuck four or five times as heavily as you want and refrigerate it overnight. The following day, tie the fennel, leek tops, carrot, celery, and parsley stems with twine. Put them, the roast, the star anise, bay leaves, and garlic into a pot large enough to fit the meat closely with several inches of space on top. Add enough water to cover by about 1 inch. Bring to a boil and lower to a simmer, skimming the scum that rises to the top.

Cook at below a simmer—there should be little water movement—adding water as needed, careful never to drown the meat, leaving only ½ inch of liquid above it, until the roast is spoon-tender, 4 to 6 hours. If serving immediately, remove to a plate and slice thickly, against the grain. Strain the broth and return it to the pot. Reduce slightly, return the sliced meat to the broth to warm, and ladle each serving copiously with broth, adding a smear of seasoned butter or salsa verde and a sprinkle of flaky salt on top of the meat. If serving another day, follow instructions for cooling and reheating boeuf à la mode (see page 187).

I have another intriguing recipe for *boeuf bouilli* from the 1905 *New Annie Dennis Cook Book*, in which one is instructed to add "a small pickled cucumber cut up fine, one anchovy, and a large spoon-ful of capers" to the beef broth, once the beef is tender. "If preferred," it allows, "they can be strained out before serving." I am too timid to try this myself . . . but why? It is sound, and someday I will do it.

There is no more honest plan for any age than *boeuf bouilli*. On the other hand, its somewhat vainglorious name aside, *boeuf à la mode* is a peasant dish masquerading as a blue blood. It is the second-simplest braised beef dish, and unique among old classics for relying on the rustic method of adding a pig's foot or veal knuckle to contribute body. (These less common cuts are more common than they sound. One or the other can be found in most butchers' cases, or just behind them. There is no preparing to do of either once you have it. It will be fresh and clean and ready to do its job.)

Here is a modern version that is easy to make. I've added the Italian condiment *gremolata*, which lifts the basic dish to new heights. An advisory note comes from a 1966 Delmonico's menu, on which *boeuf à la mode* exclaims of itself: "I must be limpid, full bodied, clear and beautiful."

BOEUF À LA MODE WITH GREMOLATA

kosher salt
1 (4-pound) chuck eye roast, in a single tied piece, if possible
1 teaspoon freshly grated nutmeg
½ teaspoon ground allspice
olive oil, for the pan
½ cup chopped or sliced onion
½ cup chopped carrot
½ cup chopped celery
1 tablespoon tomato paste
a few cloves garlic
1 (750-ml) bottle good, light-bodied red wine, or a combination
    of leftover wine to make about 3¼ cups
⅓ cup cognac or brandy
1 pig's foot or beef or veal knuckle
bouquet garni of a few sprigs of thyme and a handful of parsley
    stems
2 bay leaves
½ to 1 cup dried porcini mushrooms
2 to 4 cups beef stock

FOR THE GREMOLATA
1 cup fresh parsley, finely chopped
zest of 1 lemon, peeled with a vegetable peeler and finely
    chopped
1 clove garlic, finely chopped
flaky sea salt

A day before cooking, salt the roast very well with salt, three times as heavily as you want. Season with the nutmeg and allspice, trying to distribute them evenly. Cover with plastic wrap and refrigerate overnight.

Bring the roast to room temperature before cooking. Heat the oven to 300 degrees. In a heavy casserole, brown the meat on all sides in hot olive oil over medium heat. It should take 10 to 12 minutes. Remove the roast to a plate. Add the onion, carrot, celery, and tomato paste to the pan, scraping the bottom with a wooden spoon. Add the garlic, wine, and cognac. Cook over high heat until reduced by half. Add the roast, pig's foot, bouquet garni, bay leaves, mushrooms, and enough stock to cover the roast halfway. Cook in the oven, covered, for 3 to 4 hours, until totally tender.

If you are serving the beef the following day, allow to cool overnight in the broth, then remove the fat that has settled on top, remove the roast, warm all the braising juices, and strain through a fine-mesh sieve. If you are serving the day you cook it, remove the roast, strain the broth, and then skim the fat the best you can from its surface with a ladle.

Taste the broth. If it is acidic, add 1 to 2 cups beef stock. Adjust the salt. Remove the twine, and return the roast to the sauce until ready to serve.

To make the gremolata, *combine the parsley, lemon zest, garlic, and flaky salt to taste.*

Heat the beef in the sauce, remove to a cutting board, and slice thickly. Serve on a platter, with sauce poured over and more passed at the table, and gremolata *heavily sprinkled over everything.*

My preferred way of serving *boeuf à la mode* is surely more Provençal or, I realize, *Irish* than classic Continental. I like it best with roasted cabbage—the recipe for Everyone's Cabbage on page 112 produces a suitable specimen—or another garlicky, well-cooked bitter green, and chickpeas or some other luscious bean. If it is summer (though I doubt, with such a long-cooking dish, it is), the thinnest, most tender green beans, boiled in very salty water and tossed with olive oil or butter, would be an essentially perfect accompaniment. But, again, it probably *isn't* summer, and I must keep the two perfect companions together only in my dreams.

If a fricassee is not a sauté or a stew, and a stew after all is not

exactly a soup, then it bears saying that daube is not precisely any—
and that a *daube à la Provençal* is in a narrower category yet.

What makes a daube Provençal is its embrace of those southern
French tendencies born on the hillsides of Provence, where Richard
Olney, a true authority on what was a fricassee, a sauté, and a daube,
and how to make each in its ancient way, spent his life. His 1970 recipe for daube Provençal relies on a good deal of peasant wine and is
sweet and red with tomato; thick with garlic, thyme, oregano, summer savory, dried mushrooms, and bay leaves; fuming and rich with
pork belly, fatback, and pig skin.

No updating of a daube Provençal's flavors is necessary. It is *good*,
and tastes that way in an eternal drift. But some trims of its pro-
cesses are helpful for today's less rurally methodical human. ("With
a small, sharply pointed knife, pierce each piece of meat completely
through, with the grain, being careful not to make a wide and messy
gash. Gently force a strip of pork fat, well coated with the garlic-
and-parsley mixture, into the center of each piece of meat. . . . The
different ingredients must now be arranged in layers . . ." It goes on
for two pages.) This streamlined version still tastes of the hot French
hills, and is charming and simple.

DAUBE PROVENÇAL

2 pounds stew beef
kosher salt
⅓ cup dried mushrooms, like porcini or chanterelle
⅓ cup unsmoked bacon lardons
½ cup diced celery
½ cup diced carrot
½ cup diced fennel
½ cup diced onion
olive oil
4 cloves garlic
⅓ cup tomato paste
2 cups red wine, like Côtes du Rhone
1 whole dried chile or not very spicy fresh chile

1 cinnamon stick
1 star anise pod
a few sprigs thyme
2 bay leaves

Season the meat very well with salt, three times as heavily as you want, and leave at room temperature for 1 hour, or season the night before and refrigerate. Soak the dried mushrooms in boiling water to cover for 15 minutes, until soft. Strain through a fine-mesh sieve or coffee filter set over a bowl and reserve the liquid. Roughly chop the mushrooms.

In a large hot pan, cook the bacon, celery, carrot, fennel, and onion in a little olive oil until the vegetables wilt, then add the garlic. Cook until the vegetables are easily broken with a wooden spoon. Remove from the pan and quickly brown the meat in the same oil. Leaving the meat in the pan, deglaze with the tomato paste and red wine. Add the remaining ingredients and the mushroom soaking liquid. Bring to a boil, then lower to a very low simmer. Cook, covered, on the stove or heat the oven to 325 degrees, cooking for 2 to 3 hours, until the meat is completely tender. Taste for salt and adjust.

This daube is best with boiled potatoes, smashed with olive oil (perhaps in which a garlic clove has bubbled at some point) and a smattering of parsley or chives amid the likably starchy cloud. The *macaronade* on page 138 is an obvious and effortless plan for any sauce and bits of meat that remain in the pot after dinner.

The same gourmand who lobbied for a calf's liver recipe wants one for veal. "Osso buco. Blanc de veau. Cutlets Milanese. Stuffed Veal Breast," went her ungrammatical but heartfelt argument. But— shall I blame motherhood?—I don't eat veal often. I still eat unborn chickens, and that euphemistically named Louisiana delicacy *cochon de lait.* It is hard to get responsibly raised veal, at least where I live, and I do without. I considered searching farther afield, and then found myself reading the first line of the last chapter of Laurie Colwin's 1988 *Home Cooking*: "There comes a time in every cook's life when he or she feels he or she ought to make a stuffed breast of veal. I know this impulse well, for I have fallen prey to it . . ." And, unwilling to become prey, I abandoned further contemplation.

I offer no such objections to pork. As Grimod de La Reynière unerringly said: "*Tout est bons dans un cochon.*" ("Everything is good on a pig.") Another porcine truth comes from Richard Olney, in a recipe for his *potée aux queues et oreilles de cochon* (Boiled pigs' tails and ears with vegetables): "A pot of mustard, a dish of coarse salt, and a jar of sour gherkins [*cornichons*] should be at hand. If possible, the accompanying bread should be coarse, heavy, and not too fresh." A third truth is that many archaic pork preparations have survived and circulate with vigor today. The variety of sausages made by young butchers refreshing the old craft is abundant, and improving every year. Old breeds of pig who gain weight slowly and well have been revived and, kept by farmers who take the time to raise them, are allowed to live slow, natural, piggy lives. Everything is not only good *on* the pig, but, auspiciously for those who concur with Steinbeck that *Ad astra per alia porci, with* the pig.

Here is a recipe based on the Gascogne *garbure*, a pork-and-bean stew that dates back hundreds of years. It can be changed to accommodate taste and circumstance. It is the only dish I have eaten that manages to make of one bout of cooking three separate courses, creating an entire meal with many parts, *tous bons*. This, for a group of friends who are comfortable together, is a party dish par excellence.

GARBURE IN THREE COURSES

2 cups dried flageolet or cranberry beans
kosher salt
1 (4- to 5-pound) pork shoulder roast
2½ teaspoons fennel seeds
1 allspice berry
3 juniper berries
¼ to ½ cup olive oil
1 cup chopped leek
1 cup chopped celery
1 cup chopped fennel, plus 1 or 2 stalks fennel
⅓ cup chopped carrot
4½ cups water, broth, white wine, beer, or a combination
8 cloves garlic, unpeeled
2 bouquets garnis of thyme, parsley stems, and bay leaves
1½ tablespoons tomato paste
1 bunch kale, stems removed, leaves thinly sliced
½ head savoy cabbage, cored and thinly sliced
garnishes: coarse, heavy toast, rubbed with garlic; smooth Dijon
    mustard; cornichons
chopped fresh parsley
optional: homemade garlic mayonnaise (see page 171)

Soak the beans overnight in water to cover by 4 inches.

Salt the roast four or fives times as heavily as you want to. Grind the fennel seeds, allspice, and juniper berries and sprinkle evenly over the meat. Leave, covered, in the refrigerator overnight. The next day, heat the oven to 325 degrees. Heat a heavy-bottomed casserole with a lid, add some olive oil and the roast, and brown the roast slowly. Remove and add the leek, celery, fennel, and carrot. Add the liquid, 3 cloves garlic, 1 bouquet garni, and the roast. Bring to a bubble. Turn off the heat on the burner, cover, and cook in the oven until completely tender, 4 to 5 hours. Remove the roast from its liquid. Strain the liquid through a fine-mesh sieve, pressing on the solids. If serving immediately, put the liquid into a clean pot. If serving tomorrow, return the roast to the cooking liquid and refrigerate overnight.

Drain the beans and cover with fresh water by ½ inch. Add the fennel stalks, remaining garlic, remaining bouquet garni, and a large pinch of salt and bring to a bubble. Skim the scum that rises, lower to below a simmer, and add the olive oil. Cook until five beans are completely tender when removed from the pot and tasted—45 minutes to 3 hours. Let cool in their liquid.

To serve, heat the oven to 350 degrees. For course one, heat half enough broth to feed your group with tomato paste and 1 cup fresh water. Add the kale and cabbage and simmer until tender. Add 3 cups of the cooked beans with 1 to 2 cups of their cooking liquid. Taste the broth, adding bean liquid or water as needed, and adjust the salt. Serve the soup ladled over garlic toast, drizzled with additional olive oil if you like, topped with parsley. Leave the soup bowls on the table. For course two, warm the roast in the oven in a casserole, uncovered, with the reserved broth and a splash of water. Remove when warm to the touch and slice into thick slices, against the grain. Serve with mustard, cornichons, and garlic mayonnaise, if desired.

For course three, serve any remaining broth alongside advice that guests faire chabrol, which means "make like a goat." They must tip the wine in their glass into their soup bowls, in equal proportion to remaining broth. Forgoing spoons, they should then sip the heady elixir directly from their bowls.

When one has eaten meat so appreciatively and frugally, one's thinking rounds a theological bend. It will never be a simple matter for man to consume beasts that lived and breathed. "Some nice ragout, or charming fricassee" has a secondary effect. It recalls a truth, written once and well by Robert Farrar Capon: *that food is life, and life is good.*

AN EARLY
WINTER DINNER

Gildas

Garbure in three courses

Endives vinaigrette

Wine: A warm, savory, peppery red
Example: Syrah
Alain Graillot Crozes-Hermitage 2015

Crêpes Suzette

ON POVERTY AND OYSTERS

Seafood

VII

"It's a wery remarkable circumstance, Sir . . .
that poverty and oysters always seems to go
together."
—Charles Dickens, *The Pickwick Papers*

I know many people intimidated by the idea of cooking sea things. For anyone in this uneasy fellowship, there is no more rewarding approach than a version of the sole meunière that Julia Child called "perfectly browned in a sputtering butter sauce with a sprinkling of chopped parsley . . . a morsel of perfection . . ." Her original recipe, inevitably bound to the particulars of her culinary epiphany long ago in Rouen, provides instruction for cooking a Dover sole in clarified butter. I am sure the effect is transportive, but a close copy made with fillets of local fish in a plop of regular butter will take you very far, which is often far enough.

CRISP FISH MEUNIÈRE

4 large fillets white-fleshed fish, such as sole, scrod, hake,
    flounder
kosher salt
½ to ¾ cup all-purpose flour
1 tablespoon olive oil
7 tablespoons unsalted butter
juice of ½ lemon

½ lemon, thinly sliced into rounds and seeded
2 tablespoons chopped fresh parsley

Dry the fillets. Salt them generously. Place the flour in a large shallow dish. Dredge the fish thoroughly in the flour and shake off the excess. Heat a large frying pan over medium-high heat. Add the olive oil and 3 tablespoons of the butter. The instant the butter stops foaming, add the fish fillets. Cook for about 2 minutes, until the bottoms of the fillets are golden. Turn with a spatula and cook for 1 to 2 minutes on the second side. Remove to warm plates and tent with aluminum foil. Wipe out the pan and place over medium-high heat. Add the remaining 4 tablespoons of butter and cook for 1 to 2 minutes, until just golden. Remove from the heat, add the lemon juice, lemon slices, and parsley. Pour over the fish and serve immediately.

The guidance of Rufus Estes is handy for serving: "Fish should never be served without a salad of some kind." The salad can depend on your kitchen's inventory and your taste, more than tradition. It can be lettuce or grilled eggplant and onion, or Middle Eastern carrot and sesame. I've paired all with these delicately crisp fillets and all have been successes.

The patrician-sounding *sole grenobloise* is as simple. Make it by proceeding as though for meunière. Instead of slicing the lemon, cut it into wedges and put one on each plate. Roughly chop a tablespoon or so of capers and add them to your sputtering butter along with lemon juice in the slices' stead. Pour it over the fish and serve.

In a farmhouse outside San Sebastián, I ate a variation on *sole greno-bloise*, cooked by an ox-shouldered Basque cider maker who follows ancient ways. The ingredients are distinct from the French versions cooked fifty kilometers north along the sea, but each ingredient is represented by a shadow—butter by olive oil, lemon by vinegar, capers by garlic. The cider maker cooked this in his old wood-burning oven, with neither gauges nor knobs, and only a single fire box and iron surface above it. I have done what approximation I can in my gas oven at home.

FISH À LA BASQUE

1 large whole hake, striped bass, or sea bass
kosher salt
a lot of olive oil
cloves from ½ head garlic, thinly sliced
½ cup chopped fresh parsley leaves
½ cup apple cider vinegar
optional: Basque hard cider

Heat the oven to 400 degrees. Slash the fish skin several times and salt it heavily inside and out. On the stove, heat an oven-safe pan large enough to hold the fish. Add olive oil to thinly coat its bottom, then add the fish. Cook over high heat for 2 to 3 minutes, until the skin is crisp and the flesh whitening, then carefully turn it over and put the pan in the oven. Cook until done, 15 to 25 minutes—the exact cooking time depends on the fish. Don't be afraid to open the oven and make slits in the fish to check for doneness.

Meanwhile, heat ½ inch of olive oil in a small pan over medium heat. Fry the garlic until it has just begun to change color and remove the pan from the heat.

The instant the fish is done, remove it from the oven and add the parsley, vinegar, and the garlic-oil mixture. Carefully remove the fish to a serving dish, leaving all the juices behind. In the same pan, bring the juices to a boil and cook for about 1 minute, moving forward and back on the flame the whole time, until the sauce thickens into a light emulsion. If you can find Basque hard cider, add a pour now. The cider maker says: "Pour the sauce over the fish and serve immediately. People should be waiting for it."

Other classic fish dishes, usually sole fillets poached in wine served with a heavy sauce, seem, to my tastes, overdone, and their gradual removal from culinary habit to my mind an act of gastronomic kindness. But there is a single sauce, thick and rich as hollandaise, *sauce normande, sauce Bercy,* and *sauce Marguery*—combinations of egg yolks, butter, wine, and fish stock (and sometimes flour) that once sauced fish—that should sustain. It is prettily called *pil pil*, which means "soft bubbling," and deserves the compliment paid *sauce Marguery* by nineteenth-century epicure Diamond Jim Brady that it was so delicious he would "eat a dishrag dressed with it."

Pil pil contains no eggs, no butter, no stock, and no flour. It is thickened through careful whisking of the gelatin in cod's skin with warm olive oil. I believe that if it had sat beside *sole Marguery* on the menu at La Côte Basque, Diamond Jim Brady would have bestowed his blandishments on it. This recipe closely follows one by the chef Alex Raij.

COD À LA PIL PIL

kosher salt
4 (4-ounce) pieces skin-on cod
3 cups good olive oil, divided
4 cloves garlic, thinly sliced

Lay ¼ inch of salt in a pie plate large enough to fit the fish in one close layer. Lay the fish, skin side down, on top and season the flesh side lightly with salt, as for cooking. Cover with parchment paper and weight with heavy kitchen items, or foil-covered bricks. Leave at room temperature for 1 hour, then remove the cod, rinse off the salt, dry well, and refrigerate.

In a deep pot, large enough to fit all the fish, heat 1½ cups of the olive oil and the garlic over medium heat. The instant the garlic changes color, remove with a slotted spoon. Add the remaining 1½ cups olive oil and lower the heat to medium-low. Add the cod, skin side down, completely submerging it and keeping the olive oil below a bubble. Poach over low heat for about 8 minutes, until barely cooked and just beginning to flake. Carefully remove to a waiting plate. Let the olive oil cool for 5 minutes. Carefully pour most into a measuring cup or squeeze bottle, stopping when you see a milky substance at the bottom of the pot. Pour from here on into a mixing bowl, adding any juices that have accumulated around the cod. Literally drop by drop, whisk the warm oil into the mixing bowl, until you have a sauce like a very thin mayonnaise. Taste as you go, and stop adding oil when it tastes delicious, reserving what's left for other cooking. Sauce each piece of cod heavily and top with the fried garlic. Serve immediately, warm, not hot.

Croquettes of chicken and mushrooms, oysters and macaroni, and all manner of fish occupied dozens of pages, even whole chapters, in cookbooks like *The Boston Cooking School Cook Book, Common Sense in the Household,* and François Tanty's *French Cooking for Every Home.* Fish croquettes in particular are beloved by those who, like my grandmother, were reared on the ends of cans of salmon mixed with breadcrumbs and panfried.

The version I prefer comes from a tiny bar I know as Ricardo's, one street away from the sea on San Sebastián's shell-shaped coast. The bar's mussel croquettes provided me my first understanding of culinary nostalgia for the days in which bits of leftover fish were mixed in batter and fried in hot oil.

This calls for cooking mussels, but if you have mussels left over from *potage Billy By* (page 62) or another dish, they are a perfect substitute for freshly cooked ones.

MUSSEL CROQUETTES

2 pounds mussels, scrubbed
½ cup water
whole milk
½ onion, or 1 clean leek, finely chopped
3 tablespoons olive oil

kosher salt
1 clove garlic, finely chopped
5 tablespoons butter
1 cup all-purpose flour, plus more as needed
freshly ground black pepper
fresh parsley, roughly chopped
3 eggs, beaten
fresh white breadcrumbs or panko breadcrumbs
grapeseed or vegetable oil, for frying

Put the mussels and the water in a large pot, cover, and bring to a boil. Start checking the mussels for doneness the instant you see steam. Remove to a waiting bowl as they open; discard any that do not open after 7 minutes. Strain the broth through a fine-mesh strainer into a measuring cup. Remove the mussels from their shells and roughly chop, then drain in a sieve set over the measuring cup to add any accumulated liquid to the broth. Add enough milk to make 2 cups total liquid.

Cook the onion over low heat in the olive oil with a small sprinkle of salt, adding the garlic after a few minutes and cooking until both are soft enough to be broken with a wooden spoon. Add the butter, then the flour, and whisk well. Slowly add the milk-broth mixture, whisking the whole time, then cook over medium heat, whisking fairly consistently, until very tight, 7 to 10 minutes. Add the mussels, black pepper, and parsley and whisk at least 1 minute more. Cover a baking sheet with parchment paper, spread the mussel mixture over the parchment, and refrigerate overnight.

The following day, roll the mussel mixture into small torpedoes. Put some flour in a shallow dish, the eggs in a second dish, and the breadcrumbs in a third. Turn the croquettes in the flour, then dip in the egg wash, then roll them in the breadcrumbs. Refrigerate for 30 minutes. Heat 3 inches of grapeseed oil in a heavy-bottomed pot or deep sauté pan. When a breadcrumb dropped into the oil rises and sizzles, fry the croquettes in batches until they are evenly brown and crisp, moving them around for even browning, checking one by removing to a plate and cutting open—the mixture should be very hot and delicious inside—then removing them to a dish towel or cooling rack briefly as they are finished. Serve hot.

The old men who meet at Ricardo's to eat croquettes, make small talk, and watch Real Sociedad play soccer on a tiny television, eat them accompanied by nothing but small glasses of red wine and the rubadub of early evening. It is a fine combination, so long as the wine is dry and a little cool, and conversation nimble. Though it would hardly be acceptable at Ricardo's, I have also served these croquettes with endive salad and plates of quickly cooked dandelion greens, like those served nearby in another bar called Galicia.

Here is a different sort of croquette.

These can be made with leftover *cod à la pil pil*, or with the salt cod one finds in Caribbean or Italian or Spanish grocers, which stays good for as long as you will have it. They are even closer in spirit to the salmon croquettes my grandmother loves. A cook in her day was likely to have leftover canned salmon and béchamel sauce and cracker crumbs. Today a cook is likely to have a bit of potato. In any case, the two days it takes to soak salt cod provide ample time to find some.

SALT COD CROQUETTES

1 pound salt cod
3½ tablespoons sliced garlic, plus 1 tablespoon garlic, pounded
      to a paste with a small pinch of salt
1 cup olive oil
1 cup whole milk
1 pound cooked potatoes, riced
finely chopped fresh parsley
all-purpose flour
3 eggs, beaten
fresh white breadcrumbs or panko breadcrumbs
grapeseed or vegetable oil, for frying

Soak the salt cod in cold water for 48 hours, changing the water every 8 to 10 hours. Heat the oven to 300 degrees. Poach the cod in a covered container that fits it closely with garlic, olive oil, and milk, until completely tender, 1 to 2 hours. Remove from the liquid, reserving the liquid;

let cool, then flake the fish very carefully, making sure to remove all the bones. You should end up with about 1 cup flaked cod.

Mix the potatoes, parsley, cod, ¹/₃ cup of the poaching liquid, and the garlic paste. Chill, covered, for 1 hour, then form into croquettes and chill again. Bread and fry as on page 204.

It is *more* garlic and *more* oil, but if you like both as much as I do, a bowl of homemade aïoli is an extraordinarily good and neither expensive nor difficult complement.

If you find yourself, the following day, with some remaining potato and what is left of the oily poaching liquid from the cod, cans of good sardines and chiles will produce a midcentury-Mediterranean mutt: sardine croquettes. For these, combine 2 cups boned and flaked good sardines; 2²/₃ cups riced cooked potatoes; ¾ to 1 cup liquid from poaching salt cod or olive oil and heavy cream; 2 tablespoons puréed Calabrian chiles or dried chiles, soaked in hot water, drained, and puréed with olive oil; 2 tablespoons garlic, pounded to a paste with a small pinch of salt; olive oil as needed to make them wet enough to mix well and hold together; and salt to taste. Chill, covered, then form into croquettes. Chill again, then bread and fry as on page 204.

If you are my grandmother, or like her in any way, your tastes are not for sardines, but rather desperately for salmon and sautéed onion, which can be substituted at the same measurements and cooked the same way.

Either benefit from aïoli, if there is any left, unless, again, you are my grandmother, who wants tartar sauce from a jar. These are also perfectly delicious with wedged lemon alongside and can be eaten alone, with only sips of wine and conversation.

"To catch a clam," begins *Clams: How to Find, Catch and Cook Them,* a book that is to my mind the best on several subjects, "you must first find it." Mr. Curtis Badger, the author, is aware that he risks sounding obvious. But he has his reasons. Finding a clam entails thinking like one. Clams are so different from humans that good interspecies relations demand occasionally considering what a clam is after: a shallow, sandy substrate of the ocean floor, in a salt marsh, amid *Spartina* grasses, surrounded by other clams and a steady tidal flow.

In addition to helping you catch one, this inventory of the clam's needs also offers the crucial reminder that the domestic clam, found in saltwater columns up and down our coasts, is today, as ever, one of the best beings for humans to find, catch, and cook. Our clam population is strong. Their harvesting is gentle on the ocean floor and on their neighbors—at low tide, clams are raked by hand or shallow-dredged. Most at fish stores are farmed, and represent the rare aquaculture specimen that is beneficial to the ecosystem in which it is raised. Clams, like oysters, are filter feeders. Their insides chug along, unconsciously benevolent sieves, improving the water that moves through them. The farmed clam, bred and schooled alongside its wild kin, tastes as sweet and saline as its savage sibling.

(It is worth noting that a clam has no brain. It comprises two graceful curved shells, symmetrical and ringed, connected by a muscle. It is probably true that, as Mr. Badger attests, the phrase "happy as a clam" was invented because the simple bivalve "has only two goals in life: to eat and to have sex." And it is also true that a logical hiccup is born into the idiom: brainless as it is, the clam can't enjoy those deeply absorbing activities.)

A basic clam recipe *should* read as thriftily as Fannie Farmer's for lobster: "Lobsters. Salt." Clams' would be, "Clams. Butter." But here is some embroidery.

STEAMED CLAMS

1 pound steamer or soft-shelled clams per person
3 tablespoons butter per person

Scrub the clams well. Melt the butter. Put the clams in a large pot with a little water in the bottom, cover it, and turn the heat to high. When steam rises from beneath the cover, open it and remove the steamed clams. Discard any that do not open after 7 minutes. Drain the broth from the pot through a fine-mesh sieve into a bowl. Serve the clams, still in their shells, with the melted butter in one bowl and the broth in another. Each person should clean and dip his and her own clams.

The most steamed clams I've ever eaten in a sitting is two pounds. It was a satisfying and singular private feast, and they were both my first and second course. After eating one pound, most people have room for a bit of something else, like hot corn on the cob and Fannie Farmer's lobster. Or hot dogs or sausages with mustard and cold white wine.

A hard-shelled clam can be treated almost exactly the same way. You can do nothing else to it, and can serve it according to the same pattern, perhaps with a smattering of herbs and the end of an onion in the pot to give its liquor extra herbal savor.

Waverley Root was poet, historian, and prophet, an alliance animated by some degree of elaboration, but the connection he makes between the scallop shell and Saint James sounds to me as true as geologic record.

The rose-hued scallop was linked with Saint James (*St-Jacques* in French), he writes, because in medieval times, Galicia—where Santiago de Compostela, the end of the Christian pilgrimage, lies—was almost the only place the sweet meat was fished. Pilgrims brought shells home as proof of having made the journey. "An even more matter-of-fact story," he adds, "reminds us that the pilgrims were supposed to beg their way; the scallop shell"—those of Galicia run to about five and a half inches long—"made convenient begging bowls."

He continues. "The hopping technique of the scallop accounts for its decorative shape . . . the shell has to be light in weight but also strong, so a thin shell is reinforced by the fluting which radiates like the ribs of a fan from hinge to edge."

And who knew that the watery world was host to nearly three hundred species of scallop, all of them edible? If they are all edible, there is reason to believe that they are all delicious—as scallops seem to range from good to sublime. (For sublimity, what matters, I have learned, is that they are packed "dry," which means never soaked or left in water, which will inflate them and dilute their delicate flavor. Day boats in Maine pack them dry and send them, the day they are fished, directly to any house from which an order arrives.)

Scallops deserve their frilled and lovely French name, *coquilles St-Jacques*. In English, we reserve the French for one preparation of them—the most vulgar and tantalizing. *Coquilles St-Jacques*, traditionally as deluxe as it can possibly be, involving poaching in Champagne court bouillon and a béchamel sauce thickened with Gruyère, can also be made as this more casual variation.

COQUILLES ST-JACQUES

8 ounces button mushrooms, minced (3 to 4 cups)

2 shallots, minced

4 tablespoons (½ stick) unsalted butter

scant ¾ teaspoon kosher salt

2 tablespoons minced fresh parsley, plus more to garnish

1 tablespoon minced fresh tarragon

a squeeze of fresh lemon juice

½ cup dry white wine

½ cup clam juice

1 bay leaf

6 large sea scallops

½ cup heavy cream

Cook the mushrooms and shallots in the butter over medium heat until fully cooked, salting once the mushrooms have released all their liquid and begun to fry. Add the parsley, tarragon, and lemon juice. Divide among six oven-safe dishes or scallop shells. Bring the wine, clam juice, and bay leaf to a simmer in a saucepan. Add the scallops and cook them below a simmer for 1 minute per side. Remove and place on top of the mushrooms. Boil the wine and clam juice left in the pot until reduced to ½ cup. Add the cream and boil again until reduced to ½ cup. Set the broiler to high. Pour the cream mixture over the scallops and broil until browned on top, about 3 minutes. Scatter with parsley and serve very hot.

It is not entirely easy to serve these. They must arrive at the table in hot little dishes or shells . . . it is involved to serve anything alongside them (since if you have used a scallop shell it takes up the whole place setting, and if not, you have still needed to make a cushion for a hot dish) . . . But they are worth the clumsiness and disorder. Plus, they can be followed simply, by a substantial vegetable dish, like the truly old-fashioned potatoes Delmonico, and a large salad, and a pleasing meal will be had.

In the 1902 *Harper's Cook Book Encyclopedia* I found the clearest sentence on lobster cookery—other than Fannie Farmer's terse two words—I have seen: "Lobsters are served in several ways, but there is only one way to cook them."

You might (and *should*) say the same of crab. Lobsters must be alive when you get them, and alive when they go into a pot of boiling water. They can be killed with a knife, then boiled, but this seems unnecessarily trying for the cook and the lobster. When they emerge from the pot, they are cooked, and the outstanding question is how to serve them.

The famous lobster dishes of ages before ours featured lobsters as the subjects of necromantic rites—they were further simmered in sherry sauces, doused in cream, soused in cognac, set aflame. Lobster Thermidor, lobster Newburg, *lobster à l'américaine* all demand much *doing* even after the lobster is metaphysically and mortally done. I, for one, have never heard of a lobster's spirit awakened by the zealous rituals, and always find its meat to be irremediably deadened by them.

I have thankfully come across an older way to deal with lobster—older than Escoffier and even than Carême. I found it in a recipe for lobster loaves from Mary Kettilby's 1734 *A Collection of above Three Hundred Receipts in Cookery, Physick and Surgery: For the use of all Good Wives, Tender Mothers, and Careful Nurses.*

Here is the original:

To make Lobster-Loaves:

Pick out all the Meat of three little Lobsters, shred it a little; take a piece of Butter and brown it with Flower in a Sauce-pan; then stir in a very little Onion and Parley shred very fine, and put in a little Pepper, a spoon-full of Anchovy-liquor, three or four spoonfulls of good Gravy, three Yolks of Eggs well beat; stir all these over the Fire in the brown Butter, then put in the Lobster, and stir in a little together; Take three French Rouls, and cut a round Piece off the top of each . . . fill up the Roul with the Mixture you have prepared . . . throw it into the Pan-full of scalding Liquor: When they are crisp take them out . . .

She is half right. The only sauce but plain melted butter that elevates a lobster's sweet flesh is one in which the butter can remain unctuous and thick. I like beurre blanc, a mixture of acid, shallot, and butter, which keeps its rich uniformness as it is stirred together. Here is a less eggy and less indifferently spelled version of Mrs. Kettilby's dish.

LOBSTER WITH BEURRE BLANC

3 or 4 lobsters
¼ cup white wine
¼ cup white wine vinegar
1 shallot, minced
½ cup (1 stick) unsalted butter, cubed and chilled
a splash of heavy cream, if needed
⅓ cup mixed finely chopped fresh herbs
¼ teaspoon kosher salt, or more to taste
hotdog rolls, toasted and buttered, or buttered toast

Cook the lobsters in boiling water for 7 minutes for the first pound and 1 minute more for each additional pound. Remove and refrigerate immediately.

In a small pot, combine the wine, vinegar, and shallot and boil until almost dry. Remove from the heat and add the butter, one or two cubes at a time, returning it to the lowest possible heat when needed and then removing it again, whisking continuously. Continue until all the butter has been incorporated and you have a thick emulsion. If the emulsion threatens to break, add a splash of cream and continue. Remove from the heat when done. Add the herbs and season with the salt.

Remove the lobster meat from the shells and cut into large chunks. Warm the beurre blanc in a double boiler. Add the lobster and lightly stir through for just long enough to warm it. Taste for salt and adjust.

Serve in buttered grilled rolls, or with hot buttered toast alongside.

Shrimp scampi, whose bright star dimmed in the 1980s, is garlicky and herby and simple—maybe too simple to remember, much like the goodness of chicken soup and toast with butter.

SHRIMP SCAMPI

5 tablespoons butter
2 tablespoons olive oil
2 or 3 cloves garlic
kosher salt
½ teaspoon chile flakes
⅓ cup dry white wine
1 pound wild shrimp, peeled and deveined
juice of ½ lemon
½ cup combined chopped fresh parsley and mint

Melt 3 tablespoons of the butter in the olive oil, adding the garlic and a pinch of salt as soon as the butter begins to melt. Cook over low heat until the garlic has begun to soften. Add the chile flakes and wine and cook for 1 minute, until the wine has reduced and the liquid tastes good. Raise the heat and add the shrimp, never letting the liquid boil. Cook the shrimp until just pink on one side, then flip. Remove the shrimp to a waiting plate the instant they are pink on both sides.

Add the remaining 2 tablespoons butter to the pan and, once it melts, add the lemon juice, moving the pan vigorously for 5 to 10 seconds to emulsify the sauce. Once the sauce looks a little creamy, add the herbs. Add all the shrimp back to the pan. Turn off the heat and mix through with a spoon, being careful not to break the shrimp. Serve immediately with rice or a crisp salad or both.

I do not know if my way of making scampi improves on older ones. It is nothing out of the ordinary but, perhaps, for my additional advice: This is only worth making with wild American shrimp. Otherwise, your garlic and wine and parsley should be reserved for cooking mussels or clams the same way, and named whatever you like.

Any version is as good cold, mixed with an extra drizzle of olive oil and squeeze of lemon, eaten alone or in a sandwich, or filling a halved avocado.

It is indeed remarkable that when Sam and Mr. Pickwick breathlessly talked of oysters and economics, the poorer the place, the more abundant was the oyster house. I am satisfied that Sam was an adept social observer, but times have changed. Oysters are now the food of the rich.

Here is an adaptation of the richest oyster dish I have ever read, from the first issue of *Gourmet* magazine, published in 1941. It is no retort to Sam but would have made him quizzically say, "wery queer . . ."

FRENCH CREAMED OYSTERS

½ cup (1 stick) butter
¼ cup finely chopped celery
½ cup finely chopped leek
kosher or sea salt
1 teaspoon smooth Dijon mustard
2 teaspoons fresh lemon juice
¾ cup heavy cream
2 dozen oysters, shucked, roughly chopped, liquor strained
    through 4 to 5 layers of cheesecloth and ¼ cup reserved—
    these can be bought shucked
sherry
black pepper
1 tablespoon minced delicate herbs, like chives, parsley, or
    tarragon
buttered toast

Melt the butter in a medium-size saucepan. Add the celery, leek, and a tiny pinch of salt and cook, stirring, until tender, 7 to 8 minutes, adding drops of water if needed. Stir in mustard and lemon juice and mix well. Add the cream and ¼ cup oyster liquor. Bring to a boil, reduce to a simmer, and cook until thickened and velvety, 3 to 4 minutes. Add the oysters and cook for 2 to 3 minutes, until just firm and plump. Taste for salt, and adjust if necessary. Turn off the heat, add just a splash of sherry, and rush to the table, where hot buttered toast should be waiting, along with a bottle of cold Champagne.

This last recipe comes from George Augustus Sala's 1896 *The Thorough Good Cook*, where it is nearly hidden among such relics as Lobster Mayonnaise with Aspic Jelly, Crayfish Pudding, and Carp au Bleu au Court Bouillon. It is a fantasy, ever more appealing for its plainness.

To Cook Trout

This is the method of the woods, and in the woods I learned it. The trout must be cooked in the open air by a wood fire on the ground, or a charcoal fire in a small Boston-furnace. Clean and scale your fish; open, clean, and wash the inside; then take two small skewers, say of red cedar wood; upon each thread a piece of fat salt pork, half an inch square; with these fix the belly of the fish asunder; annex it by the tail to a twig of plant wood, which suffer to bend over the fire, so as to bring the fish opposite to the blaze; place a large biscuit or a thin slice of dry toast under the drip of the gravy; cook quickly. For a two-pound fish ten minutes will suffice; dish with the biscuit under it, and each with salt and lemon-juice, or with shrimp or lobster sauce, or a dash of Worcester or Harvey's.

Should I bother with amendments? Is it assumed that the skewers from the grocery or whittled from your backyard birch are fine, and needn't be of the more fragrant red cedar? Is it obvious that anywhere but a bonfire two pounds of fish might need more than ten minutes, and that shrimp or lobster sauce, whatever they were when Sala took them to the woods, can be replaced with whatever hot sauce you have packed in your knapsack, or no sauce at all . . . ?

I have already sapped the recipe of some of its Delphic poetry, so I will stop, stating further only that this method is good. It is more difficult than any version of sole meunière, and I suspect its results even more likely to pave a path toward gastronomic confidence and an urge for adventure.

A LATE-WINTER DINNER

Roast oysters with pepper sauce

Clam chowder

Herb salad

Bread or crackers

Wine: A richly textured, gently dry white
with generous fruit
Example: Pinot Gris
Paul Blanck Pinot Gris Classique 2014

Charlotte Russe

CRYING FOR CREAM

Desserts

VIII

The flummery cried for cream. So did we.
—Alice B. Toklas

I used to hold the puritanical view that the best thing to end a meal with was a memory of what was eaten and drunk. I have also always supported a decanter of scotch, which rounds things out with the grace of a tapering candle.

But I find, to my happiness, that I will serve old-fashioned desserts. There is in them much steeping in cream, chilling and jelling, sweetening of egg yolks, whipping of egg whites. The results are soft puddings, custards, sponge cakes layered with cream put to chill. (That is, of course, unless the opposite is true, and the entire dessert is set aflame in front of startled guests, an old habit, not authentic to any culture, but a spectacle upon which any human at all, from caveman to child to professional gourmand, will gaze with animal interest.)

Soufflés are as variable as Grandma's fruit cobbler. They may be chocolate or apricot or sour cherry, and without any change to the soufflé's internal apparatus, will be different adventures each time. It is also worth noting that by the time they are ready to eat, soufflés are half air, an appropriate makeup for a dish whose role is to be a pleasant diversion from a meal's pending culmination.

Soufflés are rare enough now for even the basics to merit revisiting. A precise picture comes from *The Oxford Companion to Sugar and Sweets*: "Soufflé has been part of the French dessert repertoire since at least the time of Vincent La Chapelle's *Cuisinier Moderne* (1733–1735) . . . Dessert soufflés can have either a cream or a fruit purée base . . . Chocolate and lemon are two of the most common flavors."

The following soufflé is my favorite kind. It embodies all the truths about soufflés and none of the myths. It has, it bears noting, neither a cream nor a fruit purée base, but an almost saintly light one of lightly sweetened egg yolks and walnuts. This is adapted from Clementine Paddleford's *The Best in American Cooking*.

WALNUT SOUFFLÉ

butter, for the pan
4 eggs, separated
6 tablespoons confectioners' sugar
1 teaspoon orange blossom water
¾ cup finely ground walnuts
2 egg whites
optional: ratafia cream (page 223) or whipped cream, for serving

Heat the oven to 335 degrees. Butter a loaf pan or 1½- to 2-quart soufflé dish. Set in the refrigerator. Put a roasting pan with hot water that fits the loaf pan or soufflé dish on the oven's middle rack.

Whisk the egg yolks until light. Add half the sugar, continue whisking, and add the orange blossom water and the walnuts. Beat all 6 egg whites with the remaining sugar until just past soft peaks. Fold in one-third of the yolk mixture to lighten, then fold in the rest in several large swoops, turning the mixing bowl. Pour into the chilled pan and place in the oven in the pan of hot water. Lower the oven temperature to 325 degrees. (The 335 degrees was to ensure the temperature doesn't fall lower.) Cook for 45 to 55 minutes, until just barely firm. Serve with cold ratafia, if you like.

This is a truly airy fairy—more form and fragrance than substance—and a fine glove for even the heaviest-handed dinners.

In late spring at Chez Panisse, where I used to cook, there were ice creams and sherbets and puddings flavored with *noyau*: the pit of an apricot or peach, split open and tasting of sweet almond. This is an antiquated habit rooted in using all the flavoring a plant offers, from stem to bud to pit, which found its apogee in the Regency-era drink ratafia. There are twenty-five different ratafia entries in *Cooley's Cyclopedia of Practical Receipts*—including ones flavored with *noyau*, with orange blossoms, violet, walnut shell, cacao nut, and coffee, and one, called *ratafia de crème*, which includes a syrup of fern leaves and heavy cream.

This last is the mother to ratafia cream. It is authentically made with fern or apricot leaves, but as I have neither, and the leaves of my cherry tree are possibly poisonous, I use bay leaves, a still old-fashioned alternative offered in the Victorian *Art of Confectionary*.

RATAFIA CREAM

1 pint heavy cream
3 tablespoons sugar
4 or 5 bay leaves
small pinch of kosher salt
3 egg yolks
a few drops of brandy

Combine the cream, sugar, bay leaves, and salt in a small pot. Bring to a boil, then turn off the heat and let steep 30 minutes. Strain.

Beat the egg yolks with the brandy. Pour a tiny bit of the warm cream into the beaten yolks to temper them, then add all the yolks into the pot with the cream. Heat over medium heat, stirring, until thickened. Chill. Serve cold.

This cream finds its truest purpose on walnut soufflé, but is also delicious over or under fresh peaches or berries.

"It is reported that a cook of Persia had his residence next to that of Muhallab b. Abi Safra and that he presented himself to prepare for him a good dish and so that he could test him; he prepared it and offered it to him; he was pleased and called it *Muhallabiyya.*" That is the creation myth, from a thirteenth-century Andalusian cookbook, for blancmange, the most fashionable sweet of all times before ours.

Muhallabia—a pounded rice, milk, sugar, and chicken pudding, whose earliest recipe comes from tenth-century Baghdad—is blancmange's predecessor. Some time in the seventeenth century, chicken was replaced by the thickener isinglass, then cornstarch or gelatin, producing a firmly set cream or milk pudding.

Blancmange is not as extinct as the absence of its name from menus leads one to believe. A current recipe for panna cotta differs only in details. In the Middle East today, you would be offered a *malabi*, which is essentially the same thing.

Here is a modern-tasting blancmange, scented with cardamom and lemon to evoke the desert sands from which its ancestor sprang.

HAZELNUT-CARDAMOM BLANCMANGE

neutral vegetable oil, for the pan
½ cup hazelnuts or almonds
1½ cups heavy cream
1 cup cold whole milk
small pinch of salt
½ cup sugar
a few drops of pure vanilla extract
3 strips of lemon zest, removed with a peeler

2 green cardamom pods, lightly smashed
1 envelope (¼ ounce) unflavored powdered gelatin

Brush a 6- to 7-inch cake pan or other mold with vegetable oil.
   Grind the nuts in a spice grinder until very fine. Combine the nuts, ½ cup of the cream, and ¾ cup milk in a pot and bring to just below a simmer over medium heat. Strain through a chinoise or sieve lined with double folded cheesecloth into a bowl. Wrap and squeeze the cheesecloth or press well with a spatula.
   Return the liquid to a pot. Add the salt, sugar, vanilla, lemon zest, and cardamom. Bring to just below a simmer, stirring to dissolve the salt and sugar. Turn the burner off. Sprinkle the gelatin over the milk in a wide shallow bowl to bloom it. Once it is bloomed, briefly reheat the milk to just below a simmer to warm. Remove the cardamom and lemon zest. Pour the gelatin into the hot milk, whisking well to completely combine. Pour into a bowl set over another bowl filled with ice and stir consistently until completely cool. Meanwhile, beat the remaining 1 cup cream to just past soft peaks. Add the cooled nut-milk mixture to the cream by folding in one-third, then another third, then the rest, which helps everything get incorporated without overmixing. Transfer to the oiled mold. Cover the surface directly with plastic wrap and chill for at least 6 hours or up to overnight before serving.

There is a lovely recipe in Lady Jekyll's 1922 essay "A Little Supper After the Play" for "Old-Fashioned Orange Jelly," which she describes as "soft and shapeless, of the colour of a blood orange, and really tasting of the fruit . . ."

This version is subtler and more ethereal. Claudia Roden writes in *The New Book of Middle Eastern Food* that a wobbly fruit jelly is called *balouza* in Arabic. She adds: "When it is served, it trembles like a jelly. It is customary for an admiring audience to compliment a belly dancer by comparing her tummy to a *balouza*."

This cool pudding is as light as a breeze and hypnotic as a pebble dropped in a pool. It is adapted from *The New Book of Middle Eastern Food*.

CHILLED FLOWER BLOSSOM PUDDING

Note: If you're nervous about unmolding this, instead of decorating the bottom of the bowl with almonds, reserve them and scatter them over the pudding in the bowl, then scoop it directly out onto plates.

¼ cup blanched sliced almonds
½ cup cornstarch
4 cups water
½ cup sugar, or to taste
3 tablespoons orange blossom water or rose water

Arrange the blanched almonds over the bottom of a wide-bottomed bowl. Mix the cornstarch with a little of the water in a medium pot to form a smooth paste. Add the remaining water and the sugar and stir, rather than whisking, until dissolved. Very slowly, over medium-low heat, bring to a boil, stirring continuously. The instant it boils, lower the heat to a bare simmer and cook, as gently as possible, stirring continuously, until the mixture thickens and coats the back of a spoon. Add the orange blossom water and cook for 1 to 2 minutes more. Pour into the waiting bowl and refrigerate, covered, for at least 4 hours. Unmold and serve directly out of the refrigerator.

It was under somberer circumstances than the word *flummery* suggests that Alice B. Toklas served the one that so cried for cream in 1939. Hers consisted of raspberry jelly, lemon juice, and gelatin, and the friend in the Resistance to whom it was served said there was no gelatin, needed for forging false papers, left in Savoie.

Flummery is otherwise another instance of something sounding like it means. It is a lighthearted molded pudding—insubstantial, delicate, lightly sweet, the sort of food that would have been served to lucky invalids in far-gone days but today makes a fetching and summery end to an early supper.

HONEY FLUMMERY

2 cups whole milk
1 envelope (¼ ounce) unflavored powdered gelatin
¼ cup cold water
2 egg yolks
¼ cup honey
2 tablespoons sugar
1 cup heavy cream, whipped
vegetable oil for greasing mold
crushed pistachios
crushed meringues (see page 233)
orange or tangerine zest

Heat the milk in a saucepan over low heat. Sprinkle gelatin over water in a wide bowl to bloom. In a small bowl, whisk together the egg yolks, honey, and sugar. Once the milk is just hot, ladle a little into the yolk mixture to temper, then add the yolk mixture to the pot of milk. Stir over very low heat until creamy. Remove from the heat and add bloomed gelatin. Transfer to a large bowl and chill if you like over a bowl of ice, until the consistency of cream.

Fold in the whipped cream and pour into a well-oiled 1½- to 2-quart mold. Chill, covered, overnight. Unmold and top with crushed pistachios, crushed meringues, and zest.

If I had been born in the era when schoolgirls were taught to cook as part of daily public education, I would have revolted and joined shop class. I might have tolerated the sewing, but I would have stomped and retched at the idea of whipping eggs.

Older and wiser, I now see the intelligence of any young person learning how to produce basic food. I believe that if every curriculum included lessons in egg boiling and herb chopping, humankind would be happier and healthier. Plus, if we had such educational priorities, we would all know how to make chocolate mousse, a fixture in home economics lesson plans.

Chocolate mousse, which dates at least to 1750, when François

Menon published recipes for *mousse à la crème* and *mousse de chocolat*, both beaten with a bundle of twigs, is a matter of melting chocolate, whipping egg whites, and, in my more luxurious than usual way, whipping cream, then combining the three and chilling the sum. It is flourless and rich, and can be satisfying in amounts down to a demitasse. I have settled on this recipe for myself, but have been satisfied with every chocolate mousse recipe I have ever tried.

CHOCOLATE MOUSSE

1 cup heavy cream
1 tablespoon confectioners' sugar
5 eggs, separated
8 ounces semisweet (70%) chocolate, in small pieces
2 tablespoons cognac or brewed coffee
tiny pinch of kosher salt
optional: flaky salt, unsweetened whipped cream

Whip the cream with the confectioners' sugar to just past soft peaks. Whisk the egg yolks in a separate large bowl until very light, 3 to 4 minutes. Melt the chocolate with the cognac in a double boiler or in a bowl set over a small pot containing 1 inch of boiling water, stirring until smooth. Remove from the heat and cool, about 5 minutes. Add the salt to the egg whites and whip to just past soft peaks. Fold the chocolate into the yolks with a spatula, mixing as little as possible, until just combined. Gently fold one-third of the whipped egg whites into the chocolate mixture to lighten, then add the remaining thirds one at a time, as in blancmange, folding minimally, alternating with the folding in of the whipped cream.

Gently smooth the mousse into a serving container or eight to ten glasses to about three-quarters full. Cover with plastic wrap and refrigerate overnight. Serve, adding a sprinkle of flaky salt and/or unsweetened whipped cream if you like.

This can be varied almost endlessly, with sweeter or bitterer chocolates, different liqueurs, and the additions of vanilla extract, or orange.

Or, more simply, follow the recipe above, omitting the cognac and/ or the cream. Whisk the yolks into the cooled melted chocolate one by one, rather than together beforehand, then beat the whites, fold them into the chocolate, and have mousse with so little work it might be called child's play.

Here is another mousse, adapted from one of the most popular dessert books of last century, Maida Heatter's 1974 *Book of Great Desserts*. It comes from a roadside beekeeper, and produces a light buttercup-yellow edifice of frozen cream that brings to mind fairy tales and enchanted forests. I can't imagine a more fantastical confection.

FROZEN HONEY MOUSSE FOR A CROWD

4 eggs, separated
2 egg yolks
½ cup honey
2 cups heavy cream
large pinch of kosher salt

In a double boiler, off the heat, beat all 6 egg yolks briefly. Move to a burner over medium heat and whisk in the honey. Once integrated, switch to a spatula and stir for 10 minutes, or until the mixture is very hot to the touch.

Remove from the heat, strain through a fine-mesh sieve, and set the custard in a bowl of ice, stirring the honey-yolk mixture until it cools. Remove from the ice bath and set aside.

In a cold bowl, whip the cream to soft peaks. In a separate bowl, whisk the egg whites with a large pinch of salt until they are just past soft peaks. Gradually fold the egg whites into half the honey, then fold the whipped cream into the rest. In a large bowl, gently fold the two together.

Gently smooth the mousse into a serving container or ten glasses to about three-quarters full. Cover with plastic wrap and freeze overnight or until firm.

Charlotte Russe emerged during First Empire France, under the name *charlotte à la Parisienne*. (The Russian charlotte is the Parisian charlotte, the name change a consequence of Carême's employ; he went to work for a tsar and paid appropriate homage.) By the second half of last century, a close copy of Carême's original—ladyfingers lining a high-sided round mold, filled with vanilla Bavarian cream and chilled—was a favorite dessert, made especially popular by the arrival on supermarket shelves of packaged ladyfingers and gelatin mixes with which to replace the Bavarian cream. Variations proliferated, and charlottes Russe appeared on dessert menus from La Côte Basque, where cream was hand whisked and savoie biscuits hand piped, to the 24-hour diner on Route 2, whose fillings may have been instant pudding or canned whipped topping, cookies from a cellophane bag, and garnishes canned peaches or strawberry pie topping. The convenience concoction left its mark, rather than the frivolous and basically simple dessert it admired. Here is how I make it.

CHARLOTTE RUSSE

2 to 3 sleeves ladyfingers
sherry
3 cups heavy cream
¾ cup sugar
5 egg yolks

1 teaspoon rose water
¼ teaspoon pure vanilla extract
2 envelopes (½ ounce) unflavored powdered gelatin
½ cup whole milk
unsweetened shredded coconut

Drizzle the ladyfingers with sherry. Line an 8- or 9-inch springform pan with parchment. Line the sides with ladyfingers, placing them closely side by side.

In a cold bowl, beat the cream and ½ cup of the sugar until the cream forms almost stiff peaks. Beat the egg yolks and remaining ¼ cup sugar on high speed until thick and pale yellow, then add the rose water and vanilla. Bloom the gelatin in half the milk in a wide, shallow bowl. Heat the remaining milk in a small saucepan over the lowest possible heat and add the gelatin, whisking well to dissolve. Once it is cool to the touch, fold in ⅓ of the egg mixture, then the remainder. Fold in ⅓ of the cream. Then fold in the remaining cream.

Fill the inside of the ladyfinger border completely with the cream filling and cover with the plastic wrap. Refrigerate for 24 hours. Uncover the top of the charlotte, then either cut down ladyfingers to unmold, or leave as they are. Unmold by placing a serving plate over the pan and inverting. Or simply release. Shower the charlotte with coconut. Serve cold.

The ladyfingers *can* be homemade and, according to your moral fiber, may even be easy. I do not know, and my moral being might not be fibrous enough to ever find out.

Tipsy charlotte or tipsy cake or tipsy parson is a simpler affair. It is a stale pound cake—which really must be stale—soaked in sherry or brandy and topped with whipped sweet cream. This is a good dessert for people who do not like to bake and those who lose track of what they buy when—and the great majority of us who by our habits if not convictions exist in the categories' overlap. Fewer people go to church today than used to. Fewer lure a parson back home with the promise of a hot meal and a tipple, and fewer yet bake a weekly pound cake. But tipsy cake is a fine reason to return to weekly baking, and may even—who knows?—summon supplicants back to the pew.

TIPSY CAKE

½ pound stale pound or sponge cake
¾ cup heavy cream
2 tablespoons fresh ricotta cheese
½ cup best-possible sweet wine (Valdinoix, Moscatel, or Sauternes)

Heat the oven to 150 to 200 degrees. Slice the cake horizontally into four layers. Stale it further in the oven for 30 minutes until very dry. In a cold bowl, whip the cream and ricotta to just past soft peaks. Lay a first layer of cake on a plate and top with one-quarter of the cream, lightly top with a second layer and more cream, then a third, more cream, and end with the final slice of cake. Reserve the remaining cream. Very slowly, allowing absorption, pour the wine over the top layer, letting it suffuse that layer and soak into the lower layers. Cover with plastic wrap and freeze for 2 to 6 hours. Cut into slices and top with the remaining cream. Serve cold.

The story of baked Alaska begins in the 1700s with the American Count Rumford, who invented the Rumford kitchen range and a double boiler, then turned to the matter of egg whites as insulation. In France, the following century, his research was applied in the creation of the *omelette norwegge*—an ice cream bombe covered in meringue and baked. Upon the U.S. acquisition of Alaska, Charles Ranhofer at Delmonico's whipped and baked such an *omelette* in the event's honor, and it was such a success that it became a menu item under the name "Alaska, Florida."

Or, in an entirely different version of the story, the *omelette norwegge* appeared much later, and Ranhofer did nothing but serve a dessert that was already as ubiquitous as mushrooms after a rain and christen it well.

In any case, the original dish was a small plain cake, filled with apricot marmalade, topped with banana and vanilla ice creams, covered in meringue, and browned. Presumably it was the tropical nature of the fruits that supplied the dessert's Floridian quality—and the baked ice cream its Alaska-ness.

It is easy to make, if a bit outlandish, if you are not attempting the highest version of it—which I believe is served in New York at Eleven Madison Park, where it has evolved into an elaborately decorated bombe that looks inedibly porcelain and tastes wonderful—but just trying to have some fun.

Here is the easy version. It is adapted from a recipe sent to me by Delmonico's, which still stands and still serves baked Alaska. It is—and yours can be—perched on cake, instead of turned onto a naked plate, as mine is, out of impatience, rather than objection.

BAKED ALASKA

1 pint best-possible vanilla ice cream, softened
1-inch-thick stale pound cake, tea cake, ladyfingers, or
   shortbread, drizzled with dessert wine to soften

FOR THE ORANGE BLOSSOM MERINGUES
3 egg whites
¾ cup superfine sugar
¼ teaspoon cream of tartar
½ teaspoon orange blossom water
optional: roasted bananas, for serving

Line a glass bowl that just fits the ice cream with plastic wrap in overlapping layers, leaving a good bit overhanging on all sides. Spread the softened ice cream into the bowl to fill. Press the cake or cookies into a firm layer, covering the ice cream and cutting to fit. Cover with the overhanging plastic wrap. Freeze until completely hard, 5 hours or up to overnight.

Heat the oven to 475 degrees. Line a flat cookie sheet with parchment paper. Unmold the ice cream by upending onto the sheet and freeze again while making meringue.

To make the meringue, whisk the egg whites to soft peaks, then add the sugar and cream of tartar by spoonfuls, continuing to whisk, until they hold stiff peaks, adding the orange blossom water near the end. Working quickly, cover the entire surface of the ice cream with meringue, frosting it with a spatula. Make sure to frost all the way to the base, so the ice cream is fully insulated. Bake on the middle or lower shelf until the meringue is browned and crisp in places, 2 to 3 minutes. Serve immediately, with sliced roasted bananas arranged around it, if you are using them, or keep in the freezer until ready to serve.

This can be bent to any whim—the ice cream can be banana, as it is at Delmonico's; it can be strawberry or pineapple or coffee. The meringues can be flavored with vanilla or almond or peppermint extract. You can make little individual Alaskas, bobbing about like snow-capped islands, or a wide flat one like a frozen plain.

If you want the meringue as cookies, rather than insulation for baked ice cream, line a baking sheet with parchment paper and pipe the meringue mixture onto it or spoon it into mounds. Turn the oven to its lowest setting and bake the meringues until just crisp, one to three hours, then turn off the oven and leave the meringues inside it several hours or up to overnight.

The orange water can be omitted or replaced with vanilla, rose, lemon, or, or, or. And the meringues can be topped with chopped almonds or pistachios or hazelnut or gold leaf, making them quite resistant to a cook's fatigue.

Surely no matter how many decades pass, children still memorize William Carlos Williams's ambivalently regretful, "I have eaten / the plums / that were in / the icebox / and which / you were probably / saving /

for breakfast . . ." But are plums still preserved and baked? They have pits in their middles from which each sweet half must be removed, and they become soft and moldy quickly. If you have your own plum tree, in your own shaded yard, the labors are worth it. But if the family tree was long ago sold, you have rhymes about plums, but no personal knowledge of plum jam and plum wine and, the category's king, plum cake.

Here is an adaptation of a plum cake baked for me by my sister-in-law with plums she had picked from the arching trees in a town near Gaillac. She adapted it from Marian Burros's justifiably famous one in the *New York Times*. It is so plummy that since first tasting it, I find myself in sympathy with Jack Horner's smug little thumb, bedecked with a plum, thinking: *What a good* (lucky) *person am I!*

PLUM CAKE

½ cup (1 stick) unsalted butter, at room temperature, plus more
     for greasing the pan
¾ cup all-purpose flour, plus more for the pan
½ cup almond flour
1 teaspoon baking powder
large pinch of sea salt
½ cup honey
½ cup plus 1 tablespoon sugar
1 teaspoon almond extract or 1 tablespoon amaretto
2 large eggs
12 smallish Italian purple plums, or 6 regular plums, halved and
     pitted
1 teaspoon fresh lemon juice
1 tablespoon sugar

Heat the oven to 325 degrees. Butter and flour a 9-inch springform pan. Sift or whisk together the flours, baking powder, and salt in a medium bowl. In a larger bowl, cream the butter, honey, and ½ cup sugar together with a handheld mixer until fluffy and light in color. Add the extract and the eggs, one at a time and scraping down the bowl, then the dry ingredients, mixing until just combined.

Spoon the batter into the prepared pan and smooth the top. Arrange the plums, skin side up, all over the batter, covering it. Sprinkle the top with lemon juice, then the sugar.

Bake for 1 hour, rotate, and continue baking until the cake is golden and a toothpick inserted into the center of the cake comes out mostly clean, an additional 20 to 30 minutes. Cool on a rack. This is even better the following day, and can be stored, covered, at room temperature.

Auguste Escoffier, who invented peaches Melba at the Savoy in 1892 (or 1893) for the soprano Nellie Melba, defended its simplicity: "a simple dish made up of tender and very ripe peaches, vanilla ice cream, and a purée of sugared raspberry. Any variation on this recipe ruins the delicate balance of its taste." Is it possible we are jaded and have forgotten the naïve magic of peach and raspberry and good ice cream? Here is a reminder.

PEACHES MELBA

4 ripe peaches
1 vanilla bean, split
½ cup plus 4 teaspoons sugar
1 cup raspberries
½ teaspoon fresh lemon juice
vanilla ice cream, softened

Put a handful of ice cubes and cold water in a bowl. Bring a large pot of water to a boil. Add the peaches and blanch until their skins seem ready to peel off, 1 to 3 minutes. Remove directly to the ice bath and leave until cool enough to touch. Peel, halve, and put in a dish with the vanilla bean. Sprinkle with ½ cup of the sugar. Cover and set aside at room temperature for 1 to 2 hours. Drain the juices from the peaches into a small pan. Warm to dissolve the sugar and pour again over the peaches. Purée the raspberries and press through a sieve into a bowl. Add the lemon juice and remaining 4 teaspoons sugar and stir. To serve, scoop vanilla ice cream into four glasses. Press 2 peach halves on either side. Drizzle with any remaining peach liquid and the raspberry sauce. Serve at once.

There may be no dessert more closely associated with late last century than crêpes Suzette. They are a lovely and very simple dessert that can be made in a straightforward fashion, sidestepping embellishments, or filled with a pageantry of Cointreau and cognac flames. Here is a no-nonsense version to which nonsense should be added at will.

CRÊPES SUZETTE

2 oranges
½ cup (1 stick) unsalted butter, at room temperature
¼ cup plus 2 tablespoons sugar

FOR THE DESSERT CRÊPES
6 tablespoons all-purpose flour
6 eggs
6 tablespoons whole milk
3 tablespoons heavy cream
unsalted butter, as needed

Zest and juice one of the oranges. Zest the second orange, saving the fruit for a snack. With a handheld or in a standing mixer, beat the butter and ¼ cup of the sugar on high speed until fluffy, about 2 minutes. Gradually drizzle in the orange juice and sprinkle in the zest, beating for about 2 minutes more. Set aside while you make the crêpes.

To make the crêpes, whisk together the flour and eggs in a medium bowl. Add the milk and cream and whisk until smooth. Pour through a strainer into a bowl and let rest for 1 hour. Heat a crêpe pan or nonstick skillet over medium-high heat until hot. Lightly butter the pan. Make the crêpes by pouring in about ¼ cup of the batter per crêpe. Stack the crêpes on a plate, separated by wax paper, or on top of one another with towels between every few, optimistically.

Melt the orange butter in a medium frying pan over medium-low heat until bubbling. Dip both sides of one crêpe in the orange butter sauce, fold it into quarters, and lay it at the perimeter of the pan. Repeat with the remaining crêpes, keeping the heat low and overlapping them around the pan. Sprinkle with the remaining sugar and broil on low for 3 minutes. Serve immediately.

And here is a shortbread recipe for easy and slightly savory cookies that gesture to the nineteenth-century habit of "savouries," or may simply be treated as timeless, for they are simple butter cookies, and sometimes needed in any age. It is adapted from Melissa Clark's.

SHORTBREAD

2 cups all-purpose flour
⅔ cup sugar
1 teaspoon plus 1 pinch kosher salt
1 cup (2 sticks) cold unsalted butter, cut into 1-inch chunks

Heat the oven to 325 degrees. In a food processor, pulse the flour, sugar, and salt. Add the butter and pulse to fine crumbs. Pulse a few more times until some crumbs start to come together, then stop. The dough should not be smooth.

Press the dough into an ungreased 8- or 9-inch square baking pan or a 9-inch pie pan. Prick all over with a fork. Bake until golden brown, 45 to 50 minutes for a 9-inch pan, 55 to 60 minutes for an 8-inch one. Transfer to a wire rack to cool. Cut into squares, bars, or wedges while still warm.

Diplomate au kirsch (à la manière de PAPAZI, as M.F.K. Fisher called it) will always exist more metaphysically than physically. There is an enchantment on the one recipe I have, from *How to Cook a Wolf,* that keeps its making elusive, skimming away when I try to nail it down. I've written my own recipe and share it with the ambivalence of a lepidopterist pinning a butterfly.

DIPLOMATE AU KIRSCH
À LA MANIÈRE DE PAPAZI 2018

1 cup mixed best-possible dried fruits, like pears, peaches,
    apricots, blueberries, cherries
¾ to 1 cup kirsch or other fruit eau-de-vie
about 20 ladyfingers
3 cups heavy cream
¼ teaspoon pure vanilla extract
⅛ cup confectioners' sugar
optional: 1 recipe *crème anglaise* (recipe follows)

Chop all the fruits to the size of the blueberries. Soak them for 45 minutes in kirsch to cover. Drain and moisten the ladyfingers with the liquid—you won't use it all. Whip the cream, vanilla, and confectioners' sugar just past soft peaks. Carefully and briskly mix the drained fruit into the cream. Line a 1½- to 2-quart charlotte mold with plastic wrap, completely covering the sides and leaving a fair amount of overhang. Line the bottom of the mold with the ladyfingers in a single layer, cutting them to fit where needed. Add a layer of the fruit-studded cream. Spread it evenly. Add a layer of ladyfingers, again fitting them tightly and cutting where needed. Press to rid of any air. Continue with the second half of the fruit and cream. Smooth the bottom and press again with a spatula to eliminate air pockets.

    Wrap the overhanging plastic wrap over the bottom of the pudding and freeze for 8 hours. Serve directly from the freezer, cut into slices, if desired, with crème anglaise *alongside.*

CRÈME ANGLAISE

2 cups half-and-half
½ cup sugar
4 large egg yolks

In a small saucepan, combine the half-and-half and sugar and bring to a simmer, whisking continuously. Cook, whisking, until the sugar has dissolved.

Set a bowl into a bowl of ice water. In another bowl, whisk the egg yolks. Very gradually whisk half the hot liquid into the yolks. Return the mixture to the saucepan and cook over low-medium heat, stirring continuously with a wooden spoon, until the sauce coats the back of the spoon, about 6 minutes. Scrape the crème anglaise *into the bowl set in the ice bath. Stir until cooled.*

When a meal has been eaten and we have had our fill, why do we ask for more? Why do we, like flummery, cry for cream?

It is, I believe, to tinge each meal with the luminescence of memory. Chateaubriand told Madame Récamier that the most beautiful half of our lives is composed of our memories. Daniel Kahneman has repeated a version of Chateaubriand's claim: our inner beings comprise remembering selves and living selves, and the remembering selves determine whether we think our lives are good.

How we store away what happens is stained or scented by an experience's final instants—and a jarring end can "ruin" a thing, though what came before remains objectively untouched.

There is no possibility of a sulfurous air hung around a dessert. It is by definition sweet. If Chateaubriand is right, we would be wise to leave things sweetly, to ensure they ripen well, since we humans, it seems, know a thing best by its end.

Something I once thought was frivolous may be practical, even stoical. What I thought was vapid may be deep. Dessert is a cook's clearest way of declaring out loud: *I will remember this well.*

ALCOHOLIC APPENDIX

A Few Drinks

IX

High spirits at the table are a vital requisite
for good digestion.

—Aldo Buzzi

This book about forgotten pleasures contains little on the subject
of food's handmaiden: drink. Scattered throughout are enjoin-
ders to drink red wine or white, or cold Pilsner, and (I believe once)
iced tea. But they are scarce.

I am no teetotaler, and the oversight was mostly that. What wasn't
a mistake was born of a belief that I should only write about things I
know well. I am a practitioner but no educator when it comes to liquid courage, aqua vitae, the wine that maketh glad the heart of man.

But I hope Aldo Buzzi's pun was intended. I agree heartily, and
know firmly that whether or not I drink well, I often end up well
drunk. I provide here, as compensation for earlier neglect, the literary
equivalent of a short bender. Should anyone need to flip back through
the text and provide alcoholic relish to courses that seem dry, he or she
can.

M.F.K. Fisher includes a recipe for what she calls "an agreeable drink
with a surprising lift to it," in *How to Cook a Wolf.* She names it
"Half-and-Half Cocktail" though it contains three halves: dry vermouth, dry sherry, and lemon juice. The three should be mixed and
poured over ice with bitters added to your taste. This is a good drink,
though I find the amount of lemon juice overbearing. I add only a
few drops—about the same amount as the bitters—and also a lemon
wedge or twist.

But even better is a drink M.F.K. herself, in life, called something like "Three-in-One." An elderly woman I once met, who claims to have known the writer well, reported that in Fisher's last days she gulped these like oxygen. They contain, to my memory, one-third gin, one-third sweet vermouth, and one-third sherry. (Or in better tribute perhaps I should say: half each of those three.) This is very like a Negroni, and a wonderful variation. More than one highball full would put most people under the table, but if one is already laid out, as Fisher was when she partook so amply of the mixture, I see no harm in several.

Here is a bit of a project, from the Vicomte de Mauduit:

Rose Liqueur Brandy

Now I shall give away my secret of how to make the most delicious liqueur in the world. You must make it in June and July, if you have, as I presume, a rose garden.

Pick eight large red roses and pluck them as directed in my recipe for rose petal jam. Be careful that no previous heavy rains have spotted any of the petals, and if the morning dew is still on them, shake out the pearly tears. Soak the petals for one month in a jar containing a quart of good cognac brandy. Cork the jar and disturb it very gently once a week.

One month later, make a syrup of three teacupfuls of best cane sugar and two teacupfuls of distilled water. Boil for twenty minute over a quick fire, then having gathered a dozen red roses and plucked them and dusted the petals with sugar, add them and bring once more to a boil, then simmer with a lid on for an hour, stirring at intervals. At the end of that time pass through a funnel fitted with a tammy into a bottle the contents of the jar, and right after the rose syrup, which you stir gently through. Stir well. Leave the bottle open (except for a piece of muslin over the opening) till the next day, to cool, then cork, shake, and seal.

I disappoint the Vicomte's presumptions. I do not have a rose garden (though my neighbors do, and have cautiously offered it to me to pick . . . one or two roses if blooms are good). Rose hips, which flower in great fat clusters all summer up and down the northeast coast, are a good replacement, and they can be picked without thought to trespassing on someone else's garden or planting your own, for they grow wild and rampant like mint or nettles, liking especially the salt air.

It is for a different time of year so probably a poor substitute for summer rose liqueur brandy, but to thank the Vicomte for his secret I shall disclose my own. This is the liqueur I believe is the most delicious in the world.

This is still made, as I understand it, in Provence today. I began making mine a decade ago in California, where citrus grows as prolifically as rose hips. It became an annual custom, and each winter I find someone willing to send me a case of bitter Seville oranges, or make do with a combination of regular oranges and regular lemons, and set a batch to rest in a cool place. It is an elixir for the ages.

HOUSE VIN D'ORANGE

2 bottles dry white wine, like Muscadet or Pinot Grigio
1 cup vodka
½ to ¾ cup sugar
½ to 1 vanilla bean, split lengthwise (this depends on how much
    you like vanilla)
1 cinnamon stick
6 Seville oranges, or 4 large navel oranges and 2 lemons,
    scrubbed and quartered

Combine everything in a big glass jar with an airtight lid. Weigh the fruit down with a bowl or glass that fits snugly inside the jar. Seal, and put somewhere cool and dark, rotating occasionally, for 4 or 5 weeks— you can always taste and decide. Taste and adjust the sugar if you like. Strain the vin d'orange through a fine-mesh sieve or cheesecloth and pour into wine or liqueur bottles or mason jars and refrigerate for up to a year.

And here is a recipe for a cocktail my husband has named "The Best Drink in the World." He chose the name because it is accurate, and because it motivates sharing its method. All one has to do is utter the sentence, "I just had the best drink in the world," to inspire the question, "What was it?" And so the formula is passed along.

BEST DRINK IN THE WORLD

1 part mescal
3 parts *vin d'orange* (page 247)
ice
Amarena cherries or homemade sour cocktail cherries

Mix the mescal and vin d'orange *well over ice. Pour over ice into a small tumbler. Top with 2 or 3 Amarena cherries, and a few spoonfuls of their liquid, to taste.*

The second-best drink in the world is made by substituting scotch for mescal; the third, by substituting rye. Bourbon can be substituted as well, but that is not the fourth best drink in the world—that is a very dry martini.

On what occasion does one drink such a concoction? We drink it in early evening, but Henry Aldrich may be helpful in providing more ideas: *If all be true that I do think / There are five reasons we should drink; / Good wine—a friend—or being dry— / Or lest we should be by and by— / Or any other reason why.*

The mescal (or scotch, etc.) can also be replaced, in the same ratio, with Champagne, or another sparkling wine. In this form, it is a good morning drink, especially by the following reasoning, reasoned very long ago by Athenaeus in *The Deipnosophists*: "If with water you fill up your glasses, You'll never write anything wise / But wine is the horse of Parnassus, That carries a bard to the skies."

In my experience, once saddled and mounted, the steed will dutifully deliver a rider to his aim, whether it is poetry, or prose, or some less canonical but equally laudable ambition. That is to say: The wine version of this drink, or any other early-day tipple, is as useful to the street cleaner as the scribbler.

The Vicomte, who has lent so many opinions and wisdoms to these pages they are scented with his own fiery philosophy, wrote: "Good food, good wines, and good alcohol do not bring about the *joie de vivre*, they stimulate it, but it must be there first in a genuine natural form." I agree. If such a natural satisfaction as he demands is hidden at dinner hour, I hope that it wakes from slumber at the sound of ice in a cocktail shaker, or the first fine taps of knife and fork against the plate, or of cool water being poured into a glass. Indeed, it matters not the flavor of the spirit's summons, only that it arrives. And that eventually, in time, it arises, renewed.

ACKNOWLEDGMENTS

The grace we say at home is comprehensive: *Thank you to everyone and everything, both present and not, that took part in bringing this meal to our table.* It covers all bases, independent of ideology. My immediate impulse is to adapt it to the current context: *Thank you to everyone and everything, both present and not, that took part in bringing this book to the page.* In this case such inclusive generality would offend, where at our wooden table it protects from offense.

I offer specific thanks to everyone and everything *not* present, because all the material for this cookbook came from the hands of people long gone.

Thank you to Kara Watson, my indefatigable editor, and to Nan Graham. Thank you to Heather Schroder, who again believed in an unlikely idea and saw it through. Thank you to everyone at Scribner, who copyedited and proofread and designed. The best part of books is when a little team is formed around them.

My brother, my mother, and my husband are my secret sources—of kitchen wisdom, of recipes, of free labor and advice, of energy, of balance, of love. I will never show them enough gratitude, but I offer all I can fit into words here. My husband, Peter, to whom this book is dedicated, deserves to share my byline. I am indebted to him for tasting each of these forgotten dishes in each of its forms, for reading paragraphs and trimming them, and most of all for repeatedly, for more than a year, putting his own ideas and projects behind mine, and for parenting, cleaning, supporting while I worked.

Samin Nosrat, Emma Tepfer, Jessica Benko, Andy Baraghani, Colu Henry, Laurie Ellen Pellicano, Rae Hellard, Treska Stein, Lenora Jane and Alé Thome, Gabriel Boylan and Christine Smallwood, Celine Nader, Heather Schroder, Benjamin Pauker, Anna Olivier, Carolyn

251

Olivier, my mother, my brother, and others I'm already forgetting helped me develop and test recipes, for which I owe them thanks.

Gideon Lewis Kraus, Jack Hitt, Ed Behr, James MacGuire, Kevin West, and Christine Jones (and again my dear Samin) helped with the messy job of cleaning up this book's writing. I slept more soundly at night knowing that their fine minds were being applied to this casual text. Thank you to Bill Wasik at the *New York Times Magazine*, who edited earlier versions of some included paragraphs, and to the *New York Times Magazine* for assigning columns on old recipes, allowing me space to find and think about them.

Thank you to my assiduous research assistant, Sophie Walker, and to the New York Public Library, where both she and I conducted hours of research in its welcoming scholars' rooms and archives. Thank you to the University of Pennsylvania's beautifully maintained Kislak Center for Special Collections, Rare Books, and Manuscripts, where I found treasures I'd never imagined.

To Mindy Dubin, who made the beautiful drawings and paintings included here, and Juliette Pope, who applied her decades of good taste to the menus' wine pairings, I am so very thankful. I am a terrible accessorizer, and without you would have sent forth my words alone on plain white pages, with little to entice.

As I was finishing these acknowledgments I felt tired of cooking and tired of writing about cooking. I wanted suddenly to do anything else for a profession, whether housepainting or winemaking or working the checkout line. I was forced to consider why I spend so much of my time cooking and writing about cooking. The answer came swiftly and drove away doubts: I love cooking for people, I love serving them meals, I love clearing away plates, pouring more wine, I love giving people I do not know my own methods for doing all those pleasurable things. I have gratitude too deep to see the bottom of to all the people I have gotten to cook for and all the people for whom I write—if it weren't for you, I wouldn't have a job and would be wandering golf courses, foraging dandelions for dinner.

INDEX

Page numbers in **boldface** refer to author's recipes.